Climbing Craftsmanship: Mastering Mental and Technical Skills


Version 1.0.04 (20191226)
Published December, 2019
Printed in the United States of America
ISBN 978-0-578-52687-4
Library of Congress Control Number:2019907928



W Won

Portland, Oregon

Inquiries, including bulk purchase discounts, permission requests, or private consultations, please address climbingcraftsmanship@gmail.com

The author hereby apologizes for the phallocentric title, but “craftspersonship” doesn’t quite roll off the tongue.

Edited and proofread by Josiah Davis (jdbookservices@gmail.com)

Cover photograph, *Twister* (.12c), Viento, Oregon, by the author

Cover design, all drawings, and interior layout by the author.

# Warning

Read this before using this book.

Climbing is an inherently dangerous sport.

You should not depend on the information in this text in regards to your personal safety. Instead, you should use your own personal judgement to assess the dangers presented to you if you choose to climb. The author cannot assure that the manner in which you climb is safe. **If you have doubt in your ability to safely ascend a climbing route, do not do it.**

The material in this book is unverified. Other climbers may have differing opinions regarding its veracity. The material in this book is not intended to prompt you to take risk. Risks such as rocks breaking or protective gear failing are inherent, and may result in serious injury or death. Moreover, belayer error, bad weather, or other acts of nature could cause serious injury or death while climbing. Before practicing the skills described in this book, be sure that your equipment is well maintained, and do not take risks beyond your level of experience, aptitude, training, or comfort level.

It is entirely up to you to engage in the sport of rock climbing. Using the information in this book to that end is entirely your responsibility.

# Acknowledgements

I appreciate the time and feedback from the various beta readers, with particular acknowledgement to Pete Johnston who continually challenged the ideas and didn't soft pedal the criticism. Pete had *significant* impact on the eventual shape of the book, helping in ways it really needed.

Mario Acosta's unflagging optimism and regular refresh of praise helped more than he knows when I found myself at wits' end, slogging through the muck. Mario kept telling me how much the material helped his climbing, pushing me to continue to polish and clarify.

Also of particular note: my son, Tristan who at turns made fun of me and edited my incessant wordiness to a dull roar, and my wife Jenn, who above all others helped in all facets of this book's production. From the early days to the very end, she kept taming my thorny prose, sometimes valiantly staying up way past her bedtime for yet another read-through.

# Climbing Craftsmanship

*Mastering Mental and Technical Skills*

# Table of Contents

# Introduction

Climbers focus a lot of time and attention on *physical training.* Hangboard routines, weight lifting regimens, and campus board efforts isolate muscles used while climbing. By focusing during these training sessions on muscles in ways that mimic climbing, astonishing gains in climbing-related strength can be realized. Training the muscles through climbing-specific exercises is a vitally important way of improving. It represents the reserve of physical energy we have at our command—what we can muster as we attempt our goals.

While there's no doubt that physical training plays a significant role in improvement, it is only one way of progressing. The ideas in this book are not opposed to physical training, it's just not the focus. Instead we look to advance ways of efficiently deploying the reserve of strength you already have through the use of skills. These skills encompass the mental, technical, and tactical aspects of the sport. Improving kinesthetic and mechanical know-how helps you improve in ways beyond increasing physical strength. Well-deployed strength results in using only the resources needed for a particular movement and no more. In this way, craftsmanship and skill progression result in movement *efficiency.*

These skills, while foundational, aren't necessarily *introductory.* As an example, we don't discuss the rudiments of hand-jams, but, instead, delve deeply into the *use the eyes* to ensure the most power from that jam. This book isn't aimed at beginners, though neophytes will profit from it, but, instead, at anyone ready to look closer at the subtleties of movement and the puzzles of the mind in the context of climbing.

*Climbing Craftsmanship* explores techniques that link the mental and technical to unlock our physical potential. Foremost in this exploration lies a pair of *meta-skills*, or skills of skills. Think of these as helpers of the psyche, enhancing in all sorts of ways. These meta-skills, when utilized attentively, help us ascend. Additionally, they produce a possibly even more important byproduct: clarity of mind, thereby reducing fear of failure and falling. These meta-skills are the origin from which other skills emerge. By investigating these meta-skills, we solidify our foundation, ensuring that the actions we take in ascent occur on a solid base. These meta-skills are particularly helpful as you can apply them at nearly every moment while you climb, and they help shape the mind optimally for the task at hand.

It's not enough, however, to know the information in this book just in your mind. You have to turn yourself into a laboratory, experimenting with and investigating what works, pushing the knowledge into your muscles. Perhaps most significantly, you must be willing to challenge your own ego and sacred cows in your exploration of the craft. Climbing with the goal of improving in this manner asks you to be honest with yourself—the most difficult of challenges. As the quantum physicist and cultural icon Richard Feynman proclaimed, "The first principle is that you must not fool yourself, and you are the easiest person to fool." Climbing often lays traps in the form of expectations and misdirections. For example, your forearms may be going nuclear, but your attention often needs focus elsewhere, particularly to your powerful lower body. Your loud and cranky forearms often divert from optimal and efficient movement. It takes knowledge and practice to counteract this tendency.

## *Combating stress and anxiety*

The skills explored in this book combat stress and anxiety. The image on the next page shows how stress can displace skill. We've all been in a position where physical exhaustion leaves us mindlessly and inefficiently pawing at holds. A few feet up a route, we look like the circle on the right, full of skill. Towards the end, as we endure the trials of climbing, we often end up like the circle on the left, with stress and anxiety just about eliminating skill. Re-engaging in skills can push the dividing line back up, displacing the stress so we look closer to the image on the right again. Stress displaces skills, but enacting skills can also displace stress. By widening and deepening the reservoir of skills, we have more tools to offset some of the stress and chatter that fills the mind. Even if it doesn't entirely eliminate the stress, it can make it more manageable.

In this book we start by exploring foundational meta-skills—the use of the eyes and breath. Using that foundation, we then shore up our base by focusing specifically on the most effective deployment of our lower body, with particular care for our feet. In addition, we investigate specific techniques to rest both our body and our mind. This helps build a toolbox of skills. Through practice, we can access that toolbox to quickly alternate from one skill to the next; we create an environment where we are too absorbed in the task at hand for fears to arise and overpower us.

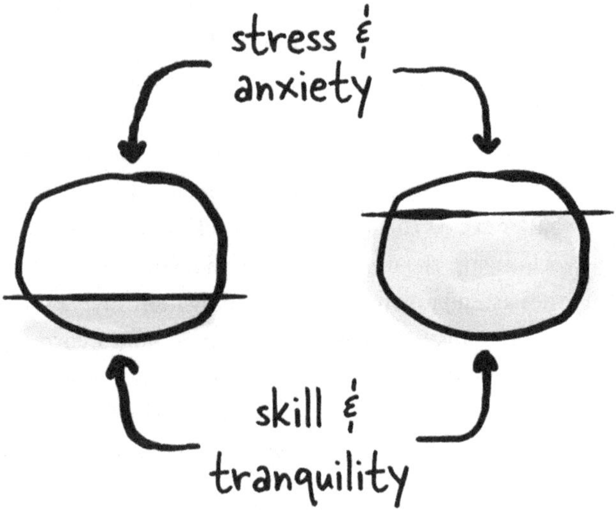


Stress and anxiety displace skill, but, conversely, mindful attention to skills can also displace stress

Practicing the meta and recovery skills presented as we continue helps deepen *tranquility*: climbing relaxed in the mind and body. To outsiders, climbing appears an extreme sport, fueled by gallons of epinephrine and testosterone. It doesn't take very long for climbers to discover a hidden secret: you almost never need more arousal, but, instead, less. Maintaining tranquility under the onslaught of climbing stress might stand as the most important skill of them all. Paradoxically, marshalling brutal power or hanging in there at the very limit of your endurance originates from a place of mental stillness. The skills and techniques presented here work to that end.

Much like regularly playing basic scales serves as the backbone for a musician to play even the most complex arrangements, and top-end professional tennis players constantly return to honing their ground strokes, practicing the information in this book can sharpen the rudiments in climbing. Through continuous practice, these skills become more available to use under times of stress, like during our hardest ascents. These skills also make our more prosaic climbs more interesting and engaging. We climb more fluidly and efficiently, harnessing our muscular reserve to maximal effect, reaping a double benefit of unlocking our physical potential while deepening the rewards of skillful execution.

## Where do I Start?

If you are relatively new to climbing, then the most important thing you can do to improve is develop a consistent schedule with at minimum two and ideally three or four sessions of climbing per week on average. Be wary of any more load, and listen to your body for the first sign of needing to dial it back. The best ability is *availability*. If you get injured, you can't practice skills or build your muscles. **Chapter 5**, with the emphasis on the lower body, is a great place to start honing your craft when you are new to the sport.

If you have some miles under your belt, but as you read this you find yourself not knowing where to begin applying this information to your own climbing, I suggest some general observations. This pointer is a vast over-generalization to take with a grain of salt. Climbers tend to fall in one of two camps. If you identify strongly with one of these two descriptions, then perhaps that may direct you to the best place to start:

- **The timid**: these sorts of climbers climb technically well but timidly, harboring inhibiting fears of failure or falling. They should spend time working on fear issues and allowing themselves to express the abilities they already have. For example, learning to use their breath and even voice while climbing (see **Chapter 3**) releases their power. Unleash the inner beast.

- **Neanderthals** are climbers with plenty of strength and enough wherewithal to will themselves past mental hurdles, but tend to do so like a bull in a china shop. This sort should spend time working on directing their focus to their lower body, learning to better engage the prime movers (see **Chapter 5**). Precisely controlling strength is key. Unleash the inner ballerina.

# Chapter 1 - The Mind

This first chapter starts the discussion of climbing with craft by investigating the mental aspects of the sport. Studying how the brain operates helps us negotiate stresses common in climbing, sharpening our edge. By becoming expert managers of the psyche, we unleash our physical strength to maximum effect.

The concept of *mindfulness* initiates the inspection of craft, a synonym for remaining vigilantly skillful at all times while climbing. Take as an example a climber, thoughtful of the details, carefully inspecting a route from the ground, notices that all of the bolts appear a left-hand clip. This attention to detail leads her to rack most of her quickdraws on the left side of her harness so that she remains efficient while hanging the draws as she ascends. While trivial, it is this very sort of skillful attention that sets the stage for success. Or, as another case in point, a climber notices three difficult left-hand moves in a row to come, so uses a marginal rest below it burning her right hand somewhat so that her left is fresh for these difficulties. Knowing yourself and paying close attention to your environment are prime attributes of mindfulness. Planning for and remaining fastidious and efficient with every movement lies at the root of craftsmanship.

In addition to the benefits of strong attention, mindfulness optimally tunes into *awareness* on the periphery as well, allowing details from intuition to percolate to the surface, and then inform movement. Instead of rigid tunnel-vision resulting from over-focus on a task, the optimally mindful climber allows the wisdom of the subconscious to assist the ascent. For example, he or she remains open to seeing options on the periphery, even when a move is underway. This open mind allows creativity and intuition to bloom.

With the basics described through this chapter, we gain solid footing to investigate the more concrete techniques later in the text. Additionally, we begin to question some of the assumptions prevalent in the sport, such as the primacy of strength, setting the groundwork for the more actionable information to come.

Mindfulness sets the foundation for a pyramid of skills. The image below illustrates the relationship of each topic in *Climbing Craftsmanship* in an ascending hierarchy with mindfulness serving as the base. Paying close attention to the skillful execution of the proficiencies described in this text helps raise your efficiency, using your physical strength optimally.

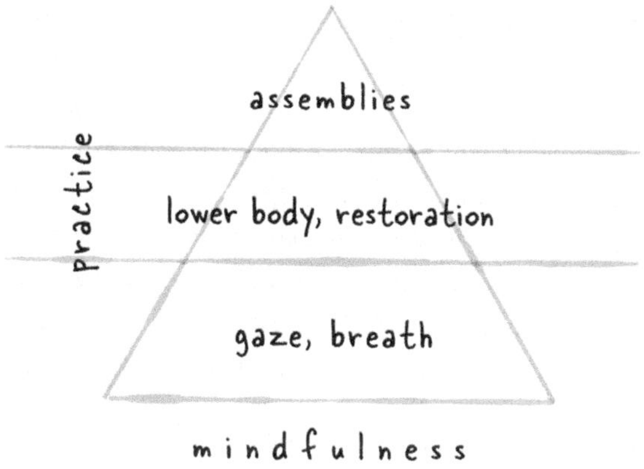


# Mental Models for Climbing

We begin the exploration of the mind through two frameworks: *Attention/Awareness* and *System 1 and 2*. These help us tease apart how the brain manages the intense workload, stimulus, and emotional barrage typical of climbing. As the book continues, we see how the application of these two models helps unleash the strength we already have.

Models help us make sense of complex phenomenon—and nothing is more complicated than consciousness. These models aren't perfect, but they help us get our arms around how we might more skillfully hone our psyche. I've paired down the two models under consideration to just the information most useful to climbing. They shed light on the mind so we can more finely tune our thinking processes during ascent. In this chapter, we introduce the concepts such that we can then get to the guts of applying the ideas in climbing. For more details of these models, see the **Appendix.**

## *Attention and Awareness*

This first theory looks at consciousness through a prism that splits it into two parts. The first, *attention*, is that of which we feel in control of in the foreground, while the second, *awareness*, represents everything in the background. To illustrate the functions of these two, imagine listening to a friend describe a captivating story. Your attention is focused on your auditory system as it interprets the sounds of her voice, turning the sounds into words and concepts. If her story is interesting enough, it tends to block out *awareness* of all other stimuli. For example, you quit feeling the itch on the back of your knee, forget about your thirst, and lose the need to answer a text message as your friend's dialog continues to focus your attention on this story to the exclusion of all else. Even though you lack consciousness of it, awareness continues to function in the background, tracking the many other perceptions that may need to override listening to your friend.

Awareness tracks all the sensory inputs not directly the focus of attention such as that itch or innumerable other tactile sensations like the feeling of your left sock on your ankle. If, however, a stimulus grows strong enough, attention may switch involuntarily to it. While listening to your friend, for example, you feel a mosquito biting your arm. Attention momentarily turns: you swat the bug, then you alternate to rapt attention on the story again. This alternation often happens with little consciousness: you might not even register that you slapped yourself. Or, sometimes, conversely, your attention will remain on the interruption. Say you suddenly remembered a critical task left undone at work while listening to your friend. You might then continue to focus internally on how to address this work situation even as your friend continues to relate her tale. Attention is but a tiny slice of all of your perceptions, thoughts, and feelings, where awareness encompasses the remainder of the pie. Thus, awareness manages the background of your life, the vast majority of sensations and input.

In climbing, the ideal balance between attention and awareness empowers our ascent. We want awareness to deliver information, overriding attention to keep us safe, and inform potential movement options. However, on the other hand, we don't want our attention hijacked by unhelpful interjections of awareness, such as fears of failure. Thus, we can improve climbing by employing skills that help turn up and down the proportion of attention and awareness in consciousness as we see fit. This book investigates nuts-and-bolts ways to this end.

## System 1 and 2

Another way to think of consciousness helpful to climbing is the System 1 and System 2 model. Here, like the previous theory, consciousness is again split into two parts: the fast, unconscious, and intuitive System 1 and the slower, analytical, and effortful System 2. These two ways of thinking have their advantages and disadvantages in climbing. Like Attention/Awareness, we can evoke one side or the other through simple techniques we inspect as the book continues.

System 1 represents the vast majority of "thinking" activities. It's the easy mentality that manages well practiced and understood activities such as riding your bike or tieing the knot into your harness after years of practice. Little to no discernible mental effort goes into such activities: they happen mostly to entirely on auto-pilot. Since most of life follows routine patterns, the mind follows established and time-worn pathways of "thinking" to accomplish goals, a strategy that works very well most of the time. You can tie your figure-eight knot while talking to your belayer, barely looking at your hands, for example.

Accomplishing System 1 goals feels "correct." It's the mentality at work when we say that "we used our intuition." When climbing straightforward terrain for our skill level, for example, we often ascend with little consciousness at all of the features or obstacles we overtake. System 1 easily pattern-matches the dozens of movement scenarios, taking action without conscious thought, and it does so efficiently and with little mental energy.

System 2, on the other hand, represents the mentality at work when System 1 can't solve the problem on its own. Tying a double bowline knot for the first few times engages System 2 thinking. It's effortful, requiring focused intention and recall from short term memory. System 2 is what we envision by the concept of "thinking:" a systematic and stepwise approach to problem solving that often results in us feeling less that a hundred percent certain we came to the correct conclusion. Again, think of tieing a knot you don't know for the first few times. It takes a lot of mental energy to recall the procedure and follow through it accurately. You feel uncertain you did it correctly until you tie it enough times to drive the skill into muscle memory.

To illustrate a climbing example of these two systems at work, say you are climbing up a route for several bolts that feels quite easy. You remain in System 1, effortlessly chugging past the moves until you find yourself unable to decipher a sequence, falling as a result. After a few more attempts trying to intuit your way through this problem, continuing to fail, you decide to carefully look at the holds at this crux, talking to yourself about the potential options: "what if I stemmed out to that right block, dropped my knee, then reached up to that side-pull? It looks like I could follow that by bumping my foot up to that ticked yoke and reach way up to the shelf." Slowing down and measuring up the moves *exactly* like this demonstrates engagement in System 2 thinking. It's analytical, procedural, slow, and trepidatious, but its careful analysis doesn't fall prey to easy mistakes like System 1. When resting on the rope, like in the scenario, or prior to starting a climb, we have plenty of time to apply demanding System 2 analysis to the problem.

Some System 2 activities, such as basic bike riding, with enough practice, turn into the domain of System 1, taking little to no conscious effort. Once we've established mastery of some tasks, they fade to the background, freeing mental resources for other uses. However, not all System 2 activities allow you to practice them to this point. Solving a complicated math problem or carefully studying a route prior to climbing it the first time requires laborious and mentally taxing analysis, carefully stepping through the process. We naturally want to avoid this, but, when we have the time, engaging in effortful System 2 analysis often unlocks movement quandaries.

As a rule of thumb, consider System 1 the primary way to approach climbing. Stay intuitive and non-analytical while moving. Only engage System 2 thought before and after climbing a route, or when at a pause large enough where you can dedicate the resources to thinking analytically. System 2 is a critical tool, *but not while moving.*

## Stress and Anxiety

With the outline of these two mental models sketched, let's turn to some other important psychological concepts, starting with details around the topic of *stress*. Climbing provokes a lot of physical and mental stimulus, commonly and collectively referred to as *stress*. However, looking closely at the term *stress* reveals nuance. By pulling it apart into subcomponents, we can investigate them in detail, revealing stress as a double-edged sword. On the one hand, we work to avoid stress as it detracts from performance, yet, on the other hand, we continually seek out stresses, for they define the challenge and ultimately transform us into a better climber as we overcome them.

- **Stressors** are events and situations that can negatively affect the climber. Fear of falling and difficult physical moves are both examples of stressors. So too is the fear of failing in front of your peer group (ego defense) or the thought of potentially missing an on-sight attempt.

- **Stress** arises when there is a perceived difference between the likely demand and your ability to respond. A stressor can result in differing amounts of stress for a climber. A V3 move for a particular climber might be just fine when attempted close to the ground, but fifty feet up, even when well protected, it could result in much more stress for the same climber.

- **Arousal** is the level of physiological and psychological activation that results from anticipated future stressors. We want the level of arousal to match the situation. Perhaps a testosterone bathed growl before a section of dynamic ape-swings is called for, or, conversely, a light, delicate, and composed state matches a slab crux. Mismatching the level of arousal to the scenario of the moment leads to inefficiency, increasing the potential for failure. Some climbers, however, like a one-trick-pony, tend to use just one level of arousal for all situations. Brutes inefficiently apply aggro to tech sequences, or polite ballerinas waste energy in their attempt to slither past a Neanderthal-ish move where just powering through makes the most sense. Learning to apply the level of arousal that is not your preferred style helps you improve.

- **Anxiety** results from the anticipation of future stressors. Anxiety is a state of mind concerned about stressors that *will* or are *likely to* occur in the future.

Put another way, stressors provoke varying degrees of stress, which in turn may increase arousal and anxiety. It's like an arrow moving from left to right: a *stressor* such as a left-hand sloper on slightly overhanging basalt stimulates a sense of *stress*. In this example, we internally sense our ability to manage this hold, adapting to the demands. This adaptation process may aggravate *anxiety* over performance. Struggling to maintain the current sloper may provoke negative thoughts about the climb that remains. Note that a *stressor* is typically, but not always, something felt in the body in real-time. At the moment, we feel sensations like pump or the lack of friction from a slippery sloper hold. On the other hand, *anxiety* is a mental response to this stimulus anticipated *in the future*. This time component is essential, because, as we will see, it's a fissure in the seeming monolithic problem of fear that we can pry open to our advantage.

Climbing often hosts inevitable stressors that we both choose and mostly (on some level) desire. Stressors are unavoidable. When we elect to climb, we select a challenge. We implicitly want at least *some* of the stressors, for they provoke the feelings of success and accomplishment, otherwise, why get off the couch?

## *Anxiety is likely the problem, not stress*

Anxiety is the sum of external stimulus and your personal history, mentally projecting a likely future outcome. Part of you, when anxious, believes the quick prognostication of the future may bode ill. For example, if you put your hand on a hold and find it is a tenuous sloper, resulting in a stressor—the thought might be, "my hand may slip off this hold if I pull hard on it." The mind nearly instantaneously compares this to a similar stimuli from the past. You struggled and often failed on previous sloper holds, giving the sensation in your body like this current one. The fast-acting subconscious, therefore, calculates failure, resulting in the emotion of anxiety. Sometimes the anxiety is a reasonable and accurate determination of the future, but sometimes it isn't: your mind's quick evaluation shortchanges you.

While we rely on the fast-acting subconscious to direct decisions, it should not be the only fact that we use in deciding how to proceed. Sometimes in climbing, paradoxically, the speedy subconscious's snap-judgment about a stimulus *causes* the expected outcome. In this sloper example, the powerful feeling of insecurity gripping the hold leads to the climber not even trying to pull the move: he or she simply unquestioningly accepts the singular prognostication arising from the subconscious as fact. Yet, this feeling of insecurity is simply the quick short-hand of the intuitions algorithm comparing history to the current stimulus. While it's often correct, it's not by any means foolproof.

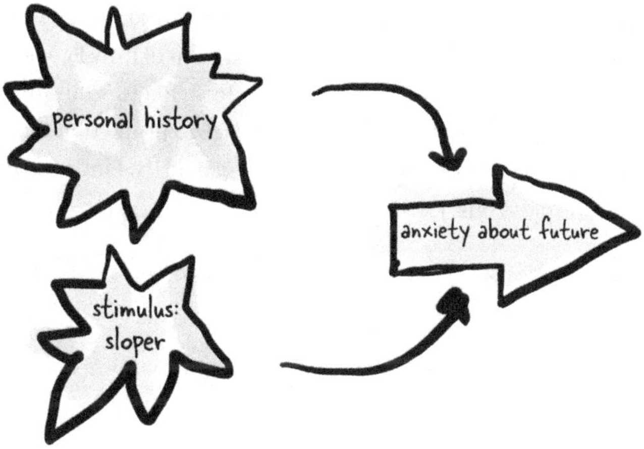


While we commonly discuss stress in climbing, it's often *anxiety* that is the more significant issue. It represents a reaction to a stimulus that may inhibit performance. We tend to pause and second guess ourselves as anxiety over the future arises. This leads to a self-fulfilling prophecy: the loss of a precious second or two as we wrestle with anxiety results in enough depletion of physical and mental resources to *cause* failure. We reach up to the sloper and feel the sense of insecurity as we attempt to find a balance point below it that works: *stress.* The moment we then turn our attention to moving past it: *anxiety.* Stress is an *in the moment* reaction to stimulus. It's what makes climbing rewarding, challenging, and enjoyable. Our mind sometimes responds maladaptively to stress as it recalls similar past experiences to project a likely outcome in the future, transforming the stress to a partially or wholly fabricated anxiety.

We certainly don't want to extinguish all anxiety out of hand. It's a highly evolved mechanism that informs our decision-making process in terms of real and perceived safety. It cautioned our ancestors on the savannah, keeping them safe from predation. It is the way our subconscious combines immediate stimulus with our historical knowledge to steer us to a future it believes safe. It is of critical importance in climbing to have this fast safety system at work in the background. Anxiety *should* be the result of proceeding into objectively dangerous terrain. We don't want to extinguish all anxieties. Instead, we want to understand them so that we can limit the damage anxieties inflict on performance.

An example of negative anxieties we want to limit are those arising out of possible ego protection. Say you are climbing with a friend you want to impress. We don't want the stress of a slippery sloper to key off anxiety based on the potential embarrassment over falling in front of him. Ego protection is the root of the vast majority of fears of failure. We form dysfunctional anxieties as an ego defense, which rarely helps. Ego protection takes many insidious forms, and these are often difficult to identify. Embarrassment in the above example is one. Here are a few others:

- Giving excuses for failures like "that foothold moved" to cover up poor performance.
- Avoiding climbing challenging routes so that others won't see if you fail.
- Using mysterious injuries as a cover story for failure.

Another anxiety is the fear of falling. When we hit that sloper and feel the stressful, non-positive discomfort, it's easy to manifest anxiety ("if I pull up on this hold, I'm going to slip off!"), even when the climbing is entirely safe. This immediate reaction of the subconscious is only one data point. It's not "truth," it's only your subconscious snap judgment. While this overly safe reaction by our subconscious to the stimulus of climbing is generally helpful, we want to impart more subtlety so that we react more in accord with the real risk. While we could fall off the sloper, it's not inevitable.

Anxieties are sometimes nearly wholly fabricated by the brain, with little objective provocation. It typically boils down to familiarity with an environment. As a case in point, consider how we can grow so anxious when climbing, even in secure situations. Many climbers become quite anxious about lead falls even when there are almost no consequences of falling. These same climbers then blithely drive home over potentially icy roads on a rainy mountain pass, at night, with questionable tires, sleepy, and checking their phone. Driving is old-hat and "safe," where climbing is "out there" and dangerous.

The fact that we fail to see the danger of cars, yet feel icy, visceral fear faced with objectively safe sport climbing falls suggests that some intuitions of the mind are somewhat irrational and perhaps at times wholly fabricated. The correlation between anxiety and objective danger is sometimes low. Climbing, by nature, provokes a heightened sense of anxiety compared to many equally or even more objectively dangerous activities.

The ruminations of the anxiety-ridden mind sometimes parallel the behavior of a misbehaving dog. Some dogs need a job at all times. If they don't have one, their idle minds turn to mischief: the stir-crazy beast misbehaves. Our thoughts are similar while climbing. If it isn't engaged in a skill, the mind is vulnerable to fears of falling and failure—it too, like a border collie, acts out. The mind, left to itself, tends to eat the couch like a stir-crazy pup. It can spin itself in a vicious cycle, with errors compounding more errors until we find ourselves in a mess of our own making.

This book presents a solution to this cushion-devouring quandary: we strengthen our mental game indirectly through the practice and application of specific mechanics. The high-frequency switching from skill to skill keeps us focused on the here-and-now: there's always a job to complete as we ascend. The mental improvements we seek are mostly derived *indirectly*—as the result of applying our attention to a specific mechanic, not from trying to be "stronger mentally." You get stronger mentally as a result, a side effect. We can't think our way out of thinking, so we need to approach rectifying problems that result from thought processes by other means, such as building an uninterrupted *chain of skills*, explored in **Chapter 6**.

Consider a few other ways to manage anxiety:

- Adding **successful events,** so our subconscious has non-negative memories to compare to a given stimulus, resulting in less and milder anxieties. Focusing on your biggest weakness and carefully adding memories of successes keeps your subconscious from protesting so loudly in the future.

- Reconditioning yourself to **interpret history differently,** so it doesn't convert negative stimulus into anxiety. Becoming less tied to ego-driven goals is an example of how you could recondition your subconscious. "Failures" are often the most significant data points that lead to growth as they signal our weaknesses. If you never fail while climbing, it suggests that you are climbing well within your ability level. Failure denotes times where you can learn something.

- Being more **mindful of the fact that anxiety is merely a mental process**, not conclusive proof. If we are aware that anxiety is just another piece of information that neither defines us nor represents an iron-clad prognostication of the future, we have more volition in how it affects us. When anxiety arises, we wrestle with it less.

- Keeping the **attention on actionable skills** at all times, displacing the space available for anxiety to roost in the mind. You do something about the situation instead of just dwelling on it.

- Practicing the **ahistorical mind**. Top athletes of all sorts cultivate a blend of denial and delusion to their advantage. It's common for top basketball players who have missed a string of shots to believe the next one is going in for sure. They tend to place the blame for misses on the external environment, not indicative of their talents, with full faith that the next opportunity will give them their due. "Pass me the ball! I'm hitting that shot!"

If you are a climber who tends to think that the reason for failure is because you aren't "good enough," experiment for a few sessions with the ahistorical mind. Every time you fail to accomplish your goal, override your natural impulse to say something like "I'm just not good enough" with a reason outside yourself: "it's too hot, and that foothold doesn't have enough friction." This helps extinguish your fabrication of how good a climber you are.

These options can all improve through practice. In a lower stress environment, we can build these skills, so our subconscious does not convert objective stress into subjective anxiety.

# Margin Call

Most climbers have more strength than required to complete their immediate goals. For many climbers, blaming strength is inaccurate and clouds priorities. The vast majority have technical, mental, and tactical problems in higher proportion to physical strength deficiencies. This isn't to say you couldn't benefit from becoming stronger. It's just likely the slowest way to improve. Adding 2% more power—a rather significant gain—but continuing to waste 20% due to inefficiencies is less effective than adding no strength but wasting only 16% of it through skill improvements. Skill weaknesses such as poor footwork for several moves in a row, over gripping due to fear of falling, or inefficient use of rests, accumulate throughout a route. These weaknesses end up putting more stress onto the comparatively tiny forearm muscles. At some point, your forearms can no longer compensate. But the reason for the failure was not the forearms—it was all of the other mistakes that required *compensation* by the poor forearms.

Another way to look at this: when we fall or take on a route, our forearms are typically screaming, "you can't go on!" It's the *proximate* (closest) cause of this breakdown. Because it is so *loud*, it's really easy to blame the forearms for the failure and thus not look at other reasons, like,

- The fact that you climbed so slowly through a section down low, spending fifteen more seconds than you needed to.
- You blew by that rest stance at the fourth clip.
- You didn't trust that slimy looking micro for your left foot and thus did not push on it maximally, pulling harder instead.
- You spent five seconds on an intricate footswitch where a slightly more powerful campus move would have spent less energy overall.

- You resisted a simple back flag because you were fearful, wasting core strength.

The accumulation of these inefficiencies that you might identify (and likely dozens more that you don't see) are the *ultimate* cause of the fall. They often remain unexplored because of how loud the *proximate* cause is. This is a fancy way of describing "the straw that broke the camel's back." It's not the last straw that did it—it's the accumulation of all of them, many of which were avoidable. Always blaming your forearms at the point of failure is like putting the last straw under a microscope, wondering how it could weigh so much more than all the others.

## *Lack of strength used as an excuse?*

Climbers tend to accept "I'm not strong enough" too quickly, before exhausting potential efficiency gains. By eradicating strength as a reason for failure, you can then start to look for other ways to improve. What else could there be? Perhaps you are not properly fueled. Are you distracted because of the new climbing partner? Did you get enough sleep the night before? Very often in climbing, failure is a version of death by a thousand cuts. We lose power through technical and mental deficiencies. Sometimes these inefficiencies are due to an apparent singular reason, such as freezing before a dyno. More often, however, multiple subtle reasons add up—such as several slightly over-gripped holds, a few foot placements that were not pushed on to their maximum, or a bobbled clip that resulted in using your left hand before the crux for three more precious seconds than necessary had you clipped it cleanly.

When you fall off a route seemingly due to pumped forearms, consider not concentrating on how to be better on the move where you failed. Instead, contemplate how you could be more efficient on the steps *leading up to that point*. When you try something hard and fail, work to replace the words "I was too pumped/weak/flamed/tired" with "I wasn't efficient enough." Blaming the failure on strength is not actionable at the moment. Focus on what kinds of things you can do *right now* to become more efficient, like,

- Relaxing deeply at the decent rest stance.
- Pushing harder on the marginal foot.

- Remaining focused on clipping the draw cleanly instead of bobbling it.

In short, replace the passive statements like "I can't do it, I'm not strong enough" or "I'm too old to climb hard" or "I'm not good at slopers" with active ones: "I will push harder with my left foot" or "I will relax deeper at the big jug at the fourth bolt." These are things that are under your control and which you can affect.

> Not blaming strength for all failures opens you up to resolving mental, tactical, or technical problems. Climbing is a skill-based sport. We need to both practice mental and technical skills **and** train strength.

Counterintuitively, when a lack of strength seems the apparent problem, you can nearly always (within reason, of course) counteract it by finding several small efficiency gains. The trick is not to allow yourself to fall prey to the first loud voice of snap judgment at the moment and instead listen to your secondary, more reflective self. While climbing, we are subject to mental processes (System 1) that are the fastest and most comfortable for our brain. We don't want to step out of this intuitive process while moving, yet the more deliberate analytical way of thinking (System 2) has a lot of insight if you learn to listen to it. We want to harvest those insights as well.

> **PRACTICE**
>
> During your next climbing session, work to eliminate any words denoting a lack of strength such as "I wasn't strong enough for that move," or "I was too pumped." Focus instead on how you could be more efficient with your energy.

You can improve your receptivity to these mental processes through the process of *reflection*. When you come down after a climb, or perhaps later in the day, thinking and talking through the technical and mental issues you encountered helps better understand the internal processes at work in climbing. The urgency of movement and the sheer volume of action in ascent precludes contemplation of subtlety while ascending. By replaying the climb in your mind with an eye towards mental processes, insight reveals itself *ex post facto*. While it's certainly true that our physical capacity plays a critical role in climbing, there's a large margin between the physical and mental parts.

Through this retrospection, you deepen your understanding of how the mind operates as the puppet master behind the curtain. This understanding helps us better counteract the negative aspects of the brain and better use the positive bits. If you have a partner that you trust, oftentimes, talking through an ascent can shed light on issues with the climb of which you may have only been dimly aware, or utterly ignorant.

## Working Through Mental Fatigue

Our ability to concentrate and focus for a sustained period plays a significant role in our physical strength and endurance. Just as our forearms get pumped, so does our ability to concentrate and focus. However, the mind is nearly silent in this regard: the energy of our will drains, but it's hard to see the decrement–it feels physical. The will to resist giving up on the terrible sloper, for example, is considerable. It also occurs at the same time our body is telling us that our grip on the sloper is very tenuous. It's, therefore, challenging to see if we fail on that hold that the most significant contributing factor was that we *just gave up*. What we may see as physical failure may be due to limitations on focus: you overcome the biofeedback from that terrible sloper through the force of attention. As the psyche tires, that force of attention wanes.

The distinction is hard to discern for two reasons: firstly, the mind does not provide easy-to-understand feedback regarding its diminishing capacity, and secondly, in climbing, most times, the mental diminishment coincides with physical exhaustion. Both happen simultaneously, yet the brain is quiet while the body is loud. This confusion casts an illusion: we think that we have a physical problem where we suffer from both a physical *and* a mental reserve problem. Sometimes the problem is one *primarily* of attention and force of will. It's difficult to spot the difference while ascending–there's too much stimulus. The issue will nearly always *seem* the result of not being strong enough. When you come down, reflect on these moments to see if you can tease out the dividing line between muscular and mental failure. The difference is often subtle, and most are conditioned not to notice. By identifying where your mind plays a crucial role in missteps, you can then identify countermeasures.

Specific kinds of routes also tend to tax our mental reserves differently than they tax our physical reserves. Scary and objectively dangerous routes demand more mental energy than their safer counterparts. Highly technical routes also tend to strain our psyche as we often feel out of balance or on the verge of falling for long time-spans. On mentally demanding routes, it's usually a good tactic to prioritize ways to rejuvenate the mental reserve. Work to become even more mindful than usual to engage in relaxation breathing (covered in **Chapter 3**) and other de-stressing tactics.

Learning how to rejuvenate and deploy the will is a skill that allows us to tap deeper into the strength we already have. When we are on the margin of our ability physically, a strong will can resist the biofeedback of exhaustion from the muscles. Often the difference between success and failure is so small that the psychic capacity to fight exhaustion is enough to succeed. Therefore, it's essential to understand the difference between mental and physical fatigue, though the two are assuredly intertwined. We want to learn how we can train our psyche to *accept* mental fatigue instead of wrestling with it. With this aptitude, we retain juice that our psyche can expend later, helping us past physical and psychological stressors up-route.

Let's look at an example to show the process of identifying and countering psychological exhaustion. In this example, Jade fails on an on-sight attempt[1] due primarily to mental problems. While, of course, this failure indelibly marks this particular route as an on-sight failure forever for her, with reflection, she can learn from this route such that her future on-sight attempts benefit. Just because she failed on this particular on-sight doesn't mean that the ascent isn't valuable to her process of improvement. Quite contrary, we harvest more information about how to improve from *failures* than *successes*. It's just hard oftentimes to ferret out actionable details when we fall that aren't reductive like "I wasn't strong enough."

---

*[1]An "on-sight" is attempting to climb a route which you have never touched and have no additional information about from the bottom to the top without falling or resting on safety gear. By definition, an on-sight attempt can only occur once per route for a given climber. There's no "second chance" with this style.*

Observe Jade as she struggles on the route, then talks through the problems with her belayer, Selena. This scene isn't the prettiest for Jade, but it's an excellent chance for her to learn about countering mental fatigue. Consider her below a two-bolt crux sequence after forty feet of climbing on-sight. She feels the exhaustion of these first forty feet while clipping the first bolt into the crux, projecting into the future few seconds that with much more movement, the fear of falling is likely to arise: anxiety. The climbing to this point has been a constant struggle with near-panic. Even at the small rest one bolt below, Jade finds herself panting for breath, unable to relax. Now, halfway through the crux, she finds herself mentally fried. While tired physically, the cumulative mental stress to this point raises a voice in her mind that since she just clipped a bolt, now would be a great time to take. This isn't the first time she's heard this inner voice on the route, but it's a lot stronger now. Her burning right forearm strongly suggests that deciding to continue or not is paramount. Part of her is very tired of fighting, of resisting the urge to hang safely on this bolt.

This example illustrates cumulative mental burnout. It's like there is an internal tally sheet kept by the mind, noting how many times we've "been good" by continuing when a sub-mind (or several) screams to stop. At some point, that internal tally sheet fills up. This phenomenon is known as *ego depletion:*[2] when you just endured a severe mental or physical trials, your capacity to engage in another one decreases. While climbing, the emotions of fear and the high levels of physical exertion cumulate to a severely depleted ego. In this state, we enter a marginal zone where success or failure of ascending one more move hangs in the balance. With each subsequent effort without recovery, our ego further depletes.

## Responding to "what if?" interjections

The mind conjures all sorts of prognostications given minimal information. These forecasts often seem a foregone conclusion. Pumped, you reach up for the two-finger pocket. It feels just at your capacity to maintain. At that moment, your subconscious raises a blurry thought to your attention: "I'm now two feet farther away from my pro! I'm maxed! What if I fall?"

---

[2]*The concept of ego depletion is debatable. Recent studies suggest that the belief in ego depletion* ***itself*** *may cause performance degradation. Willpower and self-control are likely the result of several competing and evolving agendas: you balance your desire for obtaining your goal with the need to suffer less physically, for example. It's not as simple as just forcing action through iron will as you tire.*

This anxiety, arising out of perceived danger from the subconscious, breaks the unimpeded System 1 thinking with the need for more analysis to answer the question.

We can't control when these questions arise. They arise for a range of reasons, some well justified, some wholly fabricated by the mind, with everything in between. In these moments, run through the following script:

1. Am I safe? Determining the answer to this question relies upon a set of objective and subjective reasons.

2. Yes? Switch to a meta-skill (**Chapter 2** and **3**).

# Chapter One Summary

- Anxiety is sometimes entirely a mental fabrication, projecting the past into the future.

- Climbers often overrate strength while underrating every other proficiency.

- Efficiency is as important as physical strength.

- Strength masks subtleties. As you advance through the grades, your strength no longer can compensate for deficiencies in other realms.

- Think about efficiency when you fall from exhaustion.

- Ego defense is both difficult to see and address. It can stunt growth.

- Our consciousness is composed of *attention* and *awareness*. Attention is the bit of foreground you focus on, where awareness is the remainder of the mental processing at any given moment.

- The analytic mind and intuitive body do not mix well together, but can be harnessed separately, and at the appropriate time, to significant effect.

- The mind exhausts like the muscles. You can run out of the will to enact hard physical movements if your mind is tired.

# Chapter 2 - The Gaze

In this chapter, we explore the first of two foundational proficiencies that dissipate stress and enhance precision, the use of the eyes and the skillful application of the breath. We use our eyes, for example, to engage targets. Consider this use of the eyes the *gaze,* of which there are four types discussed in this chapter. Utilizing the gaze is the first of two meta-skills discussed in this book. These "skills of skills" of which the gaze is a member are of particular use because they are *always* available as options while climbing, and have a powerful effect on the mental modes outlined in **Chapter 1**. These meta-skills help us shuttle the mind between both attention and awareness and System 1 and System 2 thinking.

## Eyes Shepherd Intention

The literal focus of our eyes marshals attention. When we want to, say, place our foot precisely on a finicky foot crystal, we both *initiate* and *carry through* the realization of this intent with our gaze solidly locked on the target. Recall the two halves of consciousness: our *attention* is what we are more directly conscious of, where *peripheral awareness* (or just *awareness* as a shorthand) is the background. We mechanically direct mental attention when we focus on targets. Thus, we escort *intent* through the skillful use of the gaze. The eyes act as a pipeline for realizing intent.

The mind will not optimally attend to your intentions when left to its own devices. Attention tends to abandon tasks just a bit before they actually complete, particularly under the pressures of climbing. The visual submind—the gaze—helps keep intent on the right track until you accomplish the mission *fully.* Put more simply: you do what you look at. If you stop looking at the components of a job—even if that job is rather trivial— it's almost certain that your attention will follow suit, resulting in mistakes. If you move your eyes to the next target too soon, you risk movement errors. Under the considerable stress of harder climbing, the mind tends to rush a bit, short-changing attention on each task, leading to errors and inefficiency.

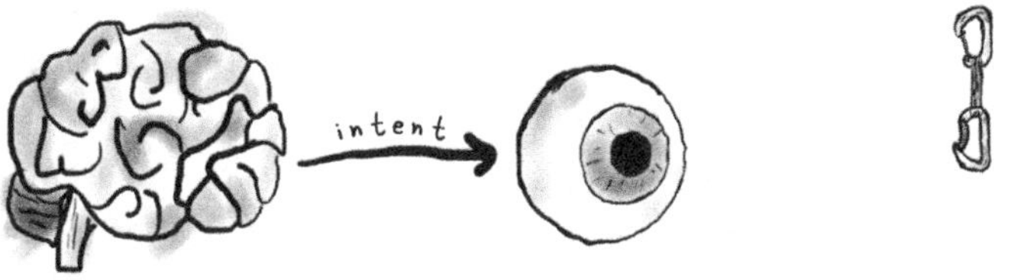


The eyes act as a conduit of intent

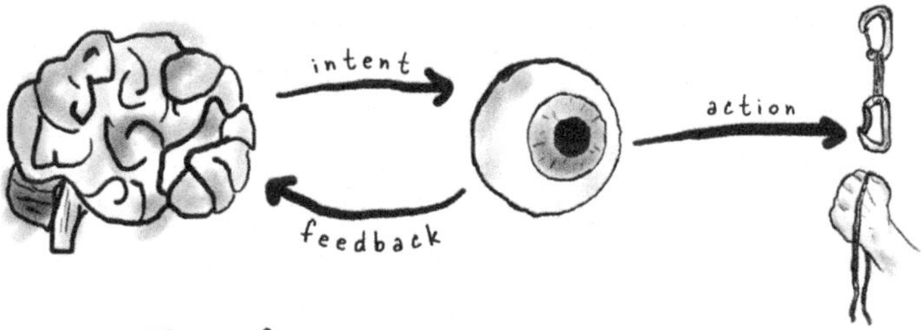


Focus of the eyes materialize this intent.
The eyes then keep the mind from wandering.

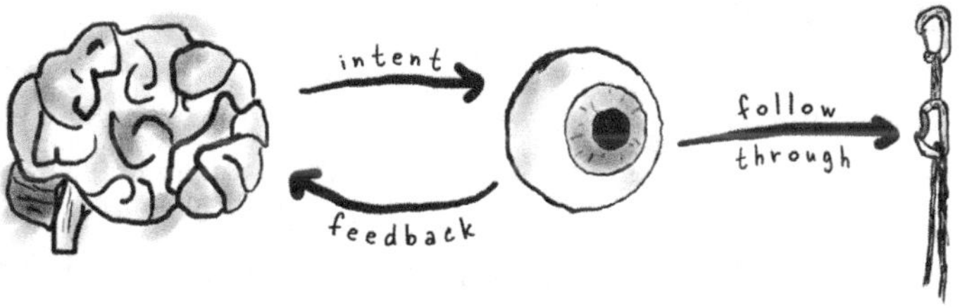


The mindful gaze shepherds intent until it's fulfilled

Choosing how to cast your gaze has significant ramifications. At the most basic level, your eyes survey the scene so that your brain can decipher your location in space in relation to the targets. Armed with this data, it determines how, *exactly*, to invoke the muscles in the precise fashion to conform to your will. If you aren't looking *specifically* at a given target, the sub-minds responsible for visually processing and then coordinating your body to make your desires a reality are disadvantaged. Try putting a key in a lock without looking closely at the keyhole: the likelihood of success is low. It takes acute visual processing and fine motor coordination to actuate this seemingly trivial mechanic successfully.

Take a climbing example: consider a small pocket that requires a perfect bulls-eye to place your toe. If you barely glance at the pocket, then look away to your next handhold while your foot is on the way, it's improbable that you end up standing on the pocket optimally, if at all. This example demonstrates how using your eyes while climbing manifests intent. Pushing as hard as possible with your lower body takes the weight off your hands. Setting the foot in optimal contact with the hold grants the best platform on which to push with your forceful trunk. You start the chain of kinesthetic events to land your foot ideally situated in the pocket by holding focus on the target while your motor system orchestrates the body to this goal. Thus, the expert use of your gaze promotes impeccable technique, discussed at length in **chapter 5**.

This example illustrates the careful deployment of exacting vision. The skillful use of our eyes, in this case, narrows down to a laser point. This acuity cuts out the background noise, providing the maximal data to solve the movement problem. This pinpoint gaze is one way to cast your eyes, which activates specific ways of thinking. In this chapter, we look at others as well.

# The Gazes

The four different *gazes*, or ways of using our vision to enable specific ways of thinking, manifest our intentions. The example above where a climber bulls-eyes a finicky pocket illustrates one, the *pinpoint* gaze, where we focus very specifically and narrowly on a target. Let's quickly outline the domain of each gaze in turn, noting how to use it to our advantage. After that, we will then look at each in detail:

1. **Regular.** This focus requires no specific work or effort as, like elastic, we unconsciously snap back to this way of seeing unless we consciously choose otherwise. While climbing, this default focus extends a few feet around us in a circle, with our eyes not typically focusing more finely than a cone of about a foot.

2. **Pinpoint.** With this gaze, we focus our eyes very precisely onto targets roughly a thumbnail in size. This is likely much more narrow than comes naturally. As an example, when clipping, the pinpoint gaze narrows down onto the carabiner right where the gate hits

the nose. The pinpoint focus provides the fine detail, which makes the skill of clipping easier and more attention-directing. We turn on our attentive brain when we focus tight on a specific target.

3. **Wide.** Focusing your vision past the immediate few moves to come defines the wide gaze. Choose this focus to turn down the attentive side of consciousness, allowing awareness to fill the void. As your awareness takes over while gazing upwards, your intuition starts to see ways of proceeding. Our subconscious sub-minds are much faster at putting together possible solutions than our conscious mind. The resultant intuitions may provide us with a treasure trove of data.

4. **Off.** We can turn off our vision by either closing our eyes (preferably), or just going blank, not looking at anything. The previous three types of gaze engage the mind. We use this engagement to lock into our ascent. However, when we find a rest stance, we may tactically choose to rest as deeply as possible. The *off* gaze fosters restoration in situations like this.

## *The "regular" gaze*

Now that we've outlined the four gazes at our disposal, let's look closely at each type, starting with the *regular* variety. The *regular* gaze is the jack-of-all-trades direction of vision, the default way of looking while climbing. It's likely, without mindful practice, that you will nearly always use the *regular* gaze. The mind has a profound preference for this sort of sight. It strikes a balance between the micro and macro focus. It's the swiss-army knife of our eyes. Most climbers focus their vision to the same resolution of about an eight-inch circle for all tasks, including,

- looking down at their gear harness for the proper cam
- scanning the next edge for the appropriate place to crimp
- looking up-route at a pause in climbing to see if they can find an option through a tricky section coming up in ten feet

Many climbers never use any other kind of gaze but this. They remain in a bubble of the same size all the time, rarely venturing outside of a few feet, and with the same resolution, regardless how close or far they look outwards.

The "regular" gaze stays in a circle about the size of our reach, with resolution of about 8"

The regular gaze isn't wrong per se, but it can be suboptimal for certain situations. We want to become proficient at understanding the purpose of each kind of gaze and when to deploy it. If the regular gaze is best for the given scenario, then we likely don't need to do anything special at all as our eyes will innately snap to that focus. However, there are many situations in climbing that benefit from different focuses. We want to use them when it helps.

The most significant advantage to the regular gaze is that you don't have to practice it—it just *happens*. If you don't need the mentality roused by the other sorts of vision, the regular gaze results in the lightest cognitive load. Its big edge is how easy it is on the mind, requiring zero effort. Its the jack of all trades, but master of none.

## *The pinpoint gaze*

This gaze is somewhat non-intuitive for climbers, so we will spend some time here spelling it out. It takes continuous practice to instill it to the point where it's available under duress. The pinpoint gaze requires mental energy. When engaging the pinpoint gaze, the brain takes more time than we think it should calculating the intricate muscle movements necessary to complete a move.

The pinpoint gaze increases attention

If we don't give our brain a *specific* target with our eyes, the movement solution won't be as precise. The pinpoint gaze tends to activate System 2 thinking slightly, so while it's a great tool to keep us ascending efficiently, it may slightly degenerate intuitive flow. For most cases, the precision and enhanced productivity are more than worth the cost but keep in mind as you experiment with this way of seeing that it's not a free lunch. It's effortful, burning some mental resource.

The "pinpoint" gaze locks down on targets the size of your thumbnail or smaller

Pinpoint focus fosters many types of precise movements. This precision also cultivates improved technique. With the small target selected, we start a movement sequence properly, encouraging ideal balance and kinesthetic advantage. Nearly every fine motor movement should begin with the pinpoint gaze.

## *Clipping via the pinpoint gaze*

Let's continue the exploration of pinpoint focus through the seemingly mundane skill of clipping a 'biner. This skill practice at once demonstrates the use of the pinpoint gaze while also engaging in the larger domain of climbing mindfully. While clipping a 'biner is a rather prosaic task, it is a great way to exemplify the use of this gaze as it's easy to describe in a way familiar to all climbers. In **Chapter 5**, we then turn what we learned here to precisely placing our feet.

When pinpointing focus with our eyes:

1. Choose the correct **specific** target. This target should be around the size of your thumbnail or smaller. This is the nose of the 'biner right where the gate hits it in the case of clipping.

2. Remain unwaveringly focused on the target while you initiate then continue the skill.

3. Keep your eye on the nose the entire time, including just a split second past completion.

4. Follow through with your eyes by keeping the gaze still locked on the target as your complete the task.

There's a set of instructions at the end of this chapter for use the next time you are out climbing or in the gym that details this information for reference as you practice. Note that while we work here on a specific case, clipping, the same aptitude is generalizable to many parts of climbing.

> Actively focus your eyes on small targets to marshal attention on specific, narrow goals. Keep your eye on that target until the mechanic is totally complete.

While practicing the clipping drill at the end of the chapter, when you come to the clipping stance, take note of your natural field of view—without practice, we tend to vaguely look at the draw with roughly an eight-inch or so circle typical of the *regular* gaze. Practice bringing your focus much tighter: laser in on the centimeter or so of the nose of the draw, right where the gate hits the nose. Notice the different experience of tightening down to the pinpoint as compared to the regular gaze.

Your subconscious needs this tight focus on a minimal area to orient itself correctly to complete the given mechanic with the highest chance of success. If your gaze is too broad, your hand is at a disadvantage when figuring out how to hit the gate. If you zero in on the nose of the draw, your body can more accurately calculate the minute mechanical motions needed to get the draw clipped. The sub-minds responsible for processing the visual information of the different components in space such as the draw, the rock face, and your limbs, orchestrate the motor system in subtle ways that are far from conscious. We help these sub-minds by precisely manifesting our intentions via the tight focus of our eyes on the *exact* target, in this case, the tip of the nose of the 'biner we intend to clip. Like finding a keyhole with your key, the pinpoint gaze is required to give the mind ample information to solve the movement problem of clipping.

Pinpoint the nose of the 'biner, right at the gate

Note that focusing attention in this way through the gaze is not the same as *thinking* about the task. We condense our intention on a target such as the nose of the 'biner, but we aren't trying to analyze the movements we need to make—that tends to activate System 2 thinking which is likely sub-optimal. Even comparatively trivial movement like clipping should remain the domain of the faster intuitive mind, System 1 thinking. We use attention focused through the eyes to direct this mindset to accomplish the goal. In doing so, we set up a more direct conduit between the body and sub-minds, keeping the analytical mind, or System 2 thinking, out of it. Focusing on specific goals is not the same as thinking analytically about them.

## Follow-through

Keep your attention on the nose of the 'biner as the rope enters it for a bit longer than feels natural, about a quarter to a half a beat. Then follow through with your eyes by keeping them on the same target until your hand fully releases. Take notice of how your focus snaps back wider as you relax your will to focus on such a small area. This helps you become more aware of that default *regular* gaze and how different it is to pinpoint down to that one centimeter.

Your eyes mobilize attention. Under stress, we tend to direct our attention to the next target too quickly. As a result, our eyes don't stay on their goal for the entirety of the mechanic. When clipping, it's common for your eyes to move away from the 'biner when your hand is *close* to the gate, but before you have *actually* clipped the draw. At that split second, your eyes and attention move to the next goal, because you assume your hand will finish the clip on its own. It's not uncommon for a bobble at that moment: the hand clipping the 'biner was off just a bit, and the rope does not make it through. As a result, you must spend the time and energy reengaging that clip. Keeping your pinpoint focus on the tip of the 'biner just that fraction of a second longer ensures your attention continues to dwell on the target long enough to complete the mechanic. Your visual sub-mind helps to keep intent on the goal for the full duration.

Thus, much like we would follow through when performing many physical activities such as shooting a basketball or a rifle, we need to practice following through the entire mechanic with climbing in general and clipping in particular. It's not that we affect the clip *after* it's complete—it's that if we don't follow through with our eyes, we unconsciously cut the mechanic short by just a split second. Following through means that you will complete its entirety with your attention affixed. We must consciously extend our focus just slightly past what *feels* like completion so that we actually *will* compete it with full attention.

Of the four different gazes discussed here, the pinpoint focus requires the most specific practice. It stands among the most critical skills considered in this book. Let's highlight the keys of the pinpoint gaze:

- **Consciously choose the exact target.** Selecting a narrow objective focuses the eyes precisely on what we want to act upon. If we don't narrow down to this precise target right on the nose of the 'biner, for example, we fall to the *regular* gaze which is too imprecise.

- **Keep your eyes on the target the entire time.** Allowing your focus to stray is easy. Stay disciplined, so your attention remains on the task at hand. On some hard moves, it's easy for your eyes to stray from the target, drifting to nowhere. Stay attentively focused.

- **Follow-through with your eyes.** Following through with the eyes until the mechanic is complete reduces errors and reinforces mastery. If you don't follow through, you will not keep your eyes on the target during the entirety of that skill.

- **Attention crowds out awareness**: Awareness allows us to process our environment at large, taking in and flagging potential options. We don't want to become so laser-focused that we lead ourselves into harm's way. Attention focuses by excluding other stimuli. An unbending exclusive focus in unfamiliar terrain could result in climbing unknowingly into a dangerous situation. The goal is not 100% focus all the time: it's directed attention when it's needed.

## *The Quiet Eye*

We've seen that mindfully approaching fine motor skills such as a clip starts with the eyes. Using the pinpoint gaze initiates precise, conscious movement. Physiologically, our eyes dance for a few milliseconds on the target as they hone down to the perfect focus. This moment where the eyes zero in is known as the "Quiet Eye" (QE). To demonstrate how QE helps precision, consider this study: researchers tracked the eye movements of athletes *in situ* via mobile eye trackers. They looked for the moment where the eye fixates within 3° or less of angle on the target for a minimum of 100 milliseconds: where the eye movements "quiet down." The highest performers in a biathlon test group demonstrated more extended QE than their lower-skilled counterparts when shooting at targets just after skiing at maximum heart rate. Elite competitors demonstrate longer duration target lock than the less skilled, particularly under duress.[1]

While it's easy to see a tennis player or other ball-sport athlete benefiting from QE, it is as important in climbing as well. The next time you climb, pay attention to how many times you, in essence, launch yourself to a target. Perhaps these movements aren't full-throated dynos or exacting

---

[1]*Hossner, E.-J. (Ed.) (2016). Quiet Eye research – Joan Vickers on target. Current Issues in Sport Science, 1:100. doi: 10.15203/CISS_2016.100*

deadpoints—the movement doesn't need to be that dramatic to have semi-dynamic elements. Each hand and foot move (and occasionally other parts of the body) acts somewhat ballistic: you look at the target and send your body part forth to land on it. Each one of these movements is like a kind of artillery firing solution sending a payload to a destination, requiring an intuitive trigonometry calculation and proprioceptive body control on the fly.

Early QE lock on a target is paramount. There's a lot of background calculation assessing your position in space and its relation to the target. It takes the brain more time than you think it should processing the information inbound from your eyes, then to formulate the complex kinesthetic solution to move your body to your goal. You improve the chances of nailing a move by locking eyes on target holds as soon as possible when using the pinpoint gaze, particularly with dynamic or semi-dynamic movements.

Obtaining QE is assisted by acquiring *specific* targets. Say you are sizing up a lunge from two small pockets to a large shelf, about a foot wide. As you look upwards to the shelf, your eyes naturally scan around the whole objective. This increases the time to QE lock. If possible, find a narrow goal, such as a small imperfection, for your eyes to latch onto, helping facilitate QE earlier.

You can practice this extended QE by modifying the clipping drill from earlier in this chapter with a half-second pause right as your hand is about to touch the 'biner. With your eye remaining focused on the nose, take note if you can of your brain acquiring QE. This sense of target acquisition is subtle but possible to detect. This drill is particularly helpful on overhanging terrain where the draw dangles in the air. It's really easy to barely touch the draw, causing your target to start spinning in space, making it that much more difficult to clip. Practice using your QE to nail clips like this perfectly. Use the little pause right where your hand is about to clip to increase the odds that the mechanic succeeds.

Unfortunately, when you are the most stressed, you are more likely to not stay focused on the objective or follow through entirely with your eyes, let alone adding a bit of QE. No matter what your ability level, under stress, you will start to regress away from your highest skill level to more primitive, untrained movements. One way to counteract this tendency is to slow down ever so slightly as you size up your next target with a QE pause. Doing so grants the mind enough time to craft the movement solution. While you want to give the brain a little more time to calculate, you don't want this to result in climbing inefficiently or like a sloth. You want to add just a quarter to a half-second to target acquisition while keeping the remainder of the movement speed high. Don't turn a brisk, flowing pace into a discontinuous, wasteful plodding to give more time to QE.

## *Wide gaze*

Like a slider control on a stereo with the bass on the left and treble on the right, sliding the lever one way increases one while simultaneously decreasing the other proportionally. When we grant attention more consciousness, awareness declines. Tightening down focus on the nose of the 'biner when clipping necessarily blocks out background awareness, just like reading these words on this page crowds out awareness of the remainder of your visual field. Don't continually channel pinpoint focus from one target to the next unless required, particularly in unfamiliar terrain such as when on-sighting.

The *wide* gaze lies at the opposite end of the spectrum from the *pin point*. Where the pinpoint gaze moves the slider to *attention*, the wide gaze shifts in the opposite direction to *awareness*. It also simultaneously turns the dial towards System 1 thinking as well. In this way, it helps us quickly assess options, becoming more open to alternatives and the intuitions of the body. Here, with no firm intention dominating, our subconscious is allowed to explore. It's much faster than our attentive side, picking up and processing many intuitions, most of which do not percolate up to the conscious mind.

PRACTICE

On routes you haven't climbed but are in the "easy" range for you, set the intention to use the wide gaze at any resting spot, looking up several moves. Allow your awareness to roam free.

With this sort of vision, we let firm attention go, ceding consciousness to the intuitive body. By doing so, the sub-minds responsible for visual pattern recognition, physical movement, and memory recall, among others, are awarded space for processing without interruption from the executive functions. This way of thinking is much faster than our analytical mode, working in ways difficult for us to make rational sense of. As mysterious as the ways of intuition might be, their subconscious results can be beneficial.

At stances with rests long enough to allow your intuitive side time to explore, activating the *wide* gaze provides a useful tool for route inspection. It sometimes provides key insights about how to proceed up-route that you would have missed if not for this switch. The relatively speedy intuitive mental mode takes on a life of its own. Imagine a dog and her master: the wide gaze, the independent dog, sleuths up-route for beta, romping to and fro—you don't control her. You hope she can ferret out details helpful to your ascent. Unlike many of the skills discussed in this book, this *wide* gaze tool is not amenable to conscious direction. You cast eyes upwards like a fisherman's net, not looking at anything in particular, hoping to reap a catch of information useful in ascent. You want potentially actionable finds for your analytical mind to plan with, but you need to keep the impatient brain from interfering with the mysterious subterranean process of intuition. Additionally, there is no guarantee that this wide net cast out for route beta will return anything of use.

The "wide" gaze looks out past the immediate few feet at nothing in particular

As if that wasn't enough, the mind tends to wander when left to its own devices. A poorly trained dog, when let loose, may start with the best of intentions, but then quickly gets sidetracked by squirrels and digging holes. Sometimes using the wide gaze results in lost focus generally, starting your mind wandering, leading to potential pitfalls such as the fears of falling or failure.

With these caveats, it's easy to see that the *wide* gaze needs careful deployment. The *wide* gaze is easily disrupted by both too much attention and too little. If we interject too much, we change our mental mode to analytical thinking, but if we don't provide enough attention to keep a fostering container around our free-form intuition, it may wander aimlessly away, wasting time. The potential benefit of deploying the wide gaze is sometimes worth the risks, as this mental mode opens a direct conduit between our perceptual sub-mind and our muscles without the clunky forebrain mucking up the works and bogging the process down.

We certainly want to know that we are heading to the right goal as we decisively execute our plan to overcome the obstacles of the climb. However, the nature of following plans devised either analytically or intuitively is that they take on their own logic. With the wide gaze, we allow our subminds to question this assumed logic freely on their own. It is this way of thinking that is likely to entertain options: maybe instead of this "obvious" jug sequence, what if we instead stem over to the right? That appears quite possible, as it leads directly to a clipping stance at the two-finger pocket. Through the wide gaze, we bring awareness and intuition to the fore, and with them, a mind less constrained by "obvious logic." The *System 1* or intuitive mode of thinking is more open and less constrained. We know that System 1, left to its own devices, is easily fooled, but intuition can often get us started down positive avenues.

> Remember to keep casting a wide field of view on unfamiliar routes when you are tired. Remember to look out to each side as well.

We often tend to start with a wide gaze which then, due to our intuition finding something of interest, naturally switches to a more analytical planning process, the domain of System 2. This initiation is a great way to use the wide gaze: it opens us up to options, the product of intuition, of which we follow up by formulating a concrete plan. The point of the wide gaze is to allow the fast awareness to take the steering wheel for a moment untethered to a lock-step schedule of movement. Once it's latched on to something, it lets the consciousness know. It's at this point then the managerial skills of attention can then evaluate the veracity of that idea, potentially formulating specific beta based off it.

If careful, we can nudge the wide gaze around a bit such that we stay in the receptive and intuitive mental mode while also lightly directing the wide gaze around the visual field. By default, the wide gaze looks mostly upwards in a cone just a few feet ahead. This zone is helpful, but we can also lightly manage the wide gaze by shifting it outside of this default field of view to reap even more information from our intuition. When the wide gaze returns with the feeling of "done," then lightly bump it to one side or farther up-route. Looking to both sides, outside of the default cone that comes naturally when we switch to the *wide* gaze is of particular importance, as there are often good options and features we didn't see on either side. Deploying this gaze opens the mind up to options and contemplation, the opposite of the panic-stricken tunnel vision.

## *Off gaze*

When we find a resting stance, we may want to use it to allow both the body and the mind to recover. Consciously turning off vision is a way to relax the sub-minds associated both with visual processing and all of that movement orchestration. We grant those neurons a repose by just turning them off. With these sub-minds on holiday, it's nearly inevitable that we become more aware of our inner-self, the state of the mind and body. The restorative breathing methods, as well as the body scan technique outlined in **Chapters 3** and **4,** are excellent skills to deploy paired with the *off* gaze. When you close your eyes, you turn your gaze inwards.

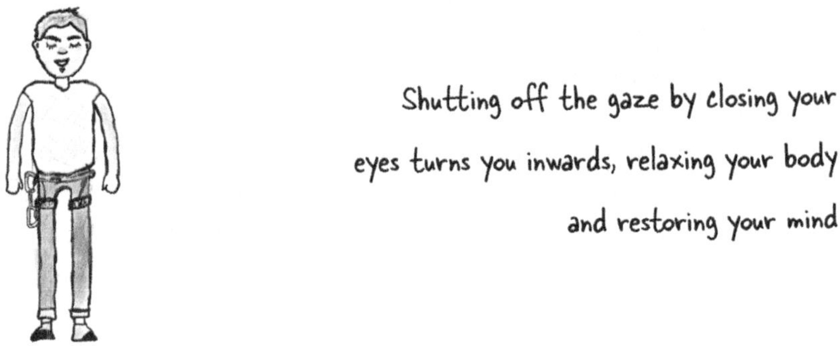


Closing the eyes, or intentionally shutting down your vision even with your eyes open with the *off* gaze, can challenge those without experience. We associate sight with being in control. It's hard to break the link between sight and safety, yet shutting down your vision is a primary way of deepening relaxation, which benefits climbing. The specialized skill of the *off* gaze is a great way to manifest the intention to rejuvenate the body and mind. This technique is typically paired with specific breathing patterns as well.

Therefore, we deepen the understanding of the *off* gaze in the next chapter when we explore the *restorative breath*, then further in **Chapter 4** with the description of the techniques of restoration.

Closing your eyes is the most powerful way of engaging the *off* gaze. However, simply intentionally allowing your visual system to "go blank" for a bit is an alternative that is often more practical. With this, you just let go of eye focus with your eyes still open, directing attention away from the world outside, allowing your consciousness to come inwards. Exhaling slowly can help this intent. As you exhale, your vision gets blurry as your attention switches from outside to in. We will delve deeper into this subject with the outline of the *body scan* technique in **Chapter 4**.

PRACTICE

On top rope, when you reach a good stance, employ the *off* gaze by exhaling slowly, allowing your vision to blur as you turn your attention inwards.

# Virtuous, Vicious Cycles

Climbing is stressful. Without consistent practice, it's likely that you will not remember to explicitly select a specific gaze. Instead you default to whatever just happens (which is nearly always the *regular* gaze). Under stress, we revert to our most basic time-worn instincts, the deepest grooves. While the *regular* gaze is sometimes the best choice, it often isn't. With increased pressure, we will start to look at the tiny pocket for our foot through the *regular* view, which is not specific enough for our visual sub-mind to reliably engage.

Looking at this tiny pocket but only tightening your focus to a one-foot circle is not precise enough, resulting in your subconscious obtaining suboptimal visual data to formulate a kinesthetic solution. This imprecision commences a vicious cycle where your inaccurate vision leads to poor target acquisition, which in turn results in poor technique as your foot lands imprecisely on the pocket. When we employ suboptimal technique, we must compensate by using more muscle, particularly from our poor, savaged forearms. The result: we burn more of our limited physical reserves.

This decrement, of course, results in more stress and with it a degradation of conscious control of your gaze for the next foot placement, leading to a landslide of inefficiency.

Purposefully choosing the correct gaze while you have some physical reserve left helps stop the avalanche, and can turn the corner so you stop burning your dwindling stamina so quickly. This commonly takes the form of forcing yourself to slow down, even while you feel on the verge of exhaustion, and pinpointing a foot placement. Manifesting your intention to act with precision via the tight focus of your eyes on a foot target can pull you back into control mentally and physically.

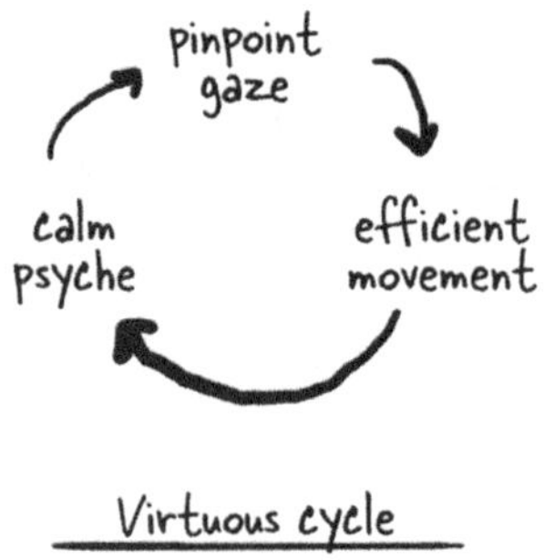


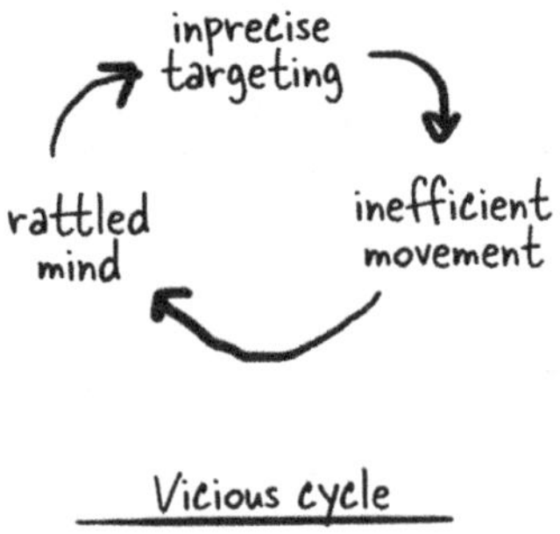


Giving short shrift to the end of a particular skill reflects anxiety about the future. If you find yourself not able to remain focused on the object for the entirety of a skill such as a clip, it's quite likely your switched unconsciously from concentrating on the present to worrying over the future. In other words, you are developing *anxiety*. This anxiety often starts a vicious cycle of losing mindfulness, resulting in poor gaze control, followed by suboptimal movement, then subsequent heightened anxiety around in a circle. Take note of this when possible, counteracting it through a renewed effort to pinpoint focus your eyes for the entirety of the mechanic, breaking the vicious cycle and returning yourself to acting on the present moment.

It's not just the *pinpoint* gaze that evaporates under high tension. Even if you practice selecting eye focus a lot, under the stress of a problematic on-sight, it's easy to fail to remember to choose the *wide* gaze towards the top of routes. This forgetfulness often results in not noticing advantageous sequences, falling victim to tunnel-vision due to the failure to look broadly.

Under extreme stress and exhaustion, selecting the correct eye focus degrades like every other skill. Practicing mindful gaze selection delays that degradation, but with enough stress, everyone reverts to their most primal patterns, eyes included. While practice partially inoculates you from this weakening of the mind, it does not cure it. However, as with most aspects of the sport, marginal improvements often mean the difference between success and failure. Being just a bit physically stronger can get you past a single move or two leading to easier terrain. Having only a bit more wherewithal through continuous practice to choose and use the correct gaze likewise unlocks opportunity on the margin. Through regular practice, we can improve our chances of staying on top of the gaze, and, thus, enhance the likelihood of success in meeting our goals.

# Chapter Two Summary

**Use your eyes to send your intent to targets. You go where you look, including inwards.**

- Our eyes send our attention to a target. We act on what we look at.
- Manifest your intention by controlling your eyes.
- Follow a mechanic through with your eyes on the target to just past when you think done, else you won't keep your eyes (and therefore attention) focused on that mechanic long enough.
- Our default field of view is often not optimal.
- Use wider angles to open consciousness to peripheral awareness.
- Use narrower fields of view to screw down attention.
- Closing your eyes turns you inwards, facilitating restoration.
- Acquire targets with your eyes as soon as possible.

## *Regular Gaze*

| Helps Facilitate | Use When |
|---|---|
| • non-demanding tasks<br>• relaxation | • the climbing is easy<br>• you need a break<br>• looking at your hands |

## *Pinpoint Gaze*

| Helps Facilitate | Use When |
|---|---|
| • attention and focus<br>• accuracy and precision<br>• manifesting intention<br>• decisiveness<br>• active movement | • clipping<br>• placing pro<br>• foot moves<br>• dynamic hand moves |

## *Wide Gaze*

| Helps Facilitate | Use When |
|---|---|
| • awareness<br>• intuition<br>• discovery<br>• openness | • at rest stances<br>• right after clipping (but not during)<br>• during *very* easy moves |

## *Off Gaze*

| Helps Facilitate | Use When |
|---|---|
| • physical rest<br>• mental restoration<br>• internal reflection | • before starting a climb<br>• at rest stances |

On a really easy route, focus 100% on the clips by employing the *pinpoint* gaze. The goal is to practice clipping, initiated through our eyes—the climbing just sets the stage. Add the stress of climbing to this drill slowly.

Your warm-up is a great time to practice. The goal here is efficient, accurate clipping through marshaling focus through the pinpoint gaze. You will climb slower than is optimal as you practice this drill, so if you get tired, just take on the rope, even if you feel a bit sheepish about taking on such an easy route.

1. As you turn your gaze to the 'biner, allow your eyes to lock on it for a quarter second before taking additional action, exploring how the *quiet eye* helps assist accuracy.

2. Keep your **eyes 100% focused** on the bottom carabiner, right where the gate meets the nose. Pause long enough with your eyes pinpointed on the nose to fully register it.

3. Keep your body dead still. **Either climb or clip.** Do not do both during this drill.

4. Exaggerate and **concentrate on reaching down** to grab the rope. Most of the time you want to keep your eye focused on the gate. If you need to move your eyes elsewhere, bring them back to the gate at the nose consciously when you can. Lock your eyes on the target.

5. Concentrate on **pulling the rope up cleanly** (to teeth or to the side).

6. Continue to **focus on the nose of the gate**, right where the gate meets it. Really zero in on that 1 cm of metal.

7. Concentrate on **flawlessly** clipping the gate.

8. Make sure you **follow through with your eyes** until the rope is cleanly sitting in on the carabiner and the gate closes.

9. Pay attention to your finger motion through the gate. **Did you clip cleanly** and exit your hand out without catching it? Were there any issues? If so, take mental note of the arrangement. Is there something about this particular situation that requires specific practice? For example, perhaps you are not proficient with left-hand clips where the gate faces away from you.

As you progress through this basic drill, here are some ideas to up the ante. Keep in mind that keeping the number of things you are practicing in one drill low is a key to success. Keep it simple, adding complexity more slowly than you think you need to.

- Clip slowly, exaggerating each step even more. Be conscious of each mechanic as you clip. This will help you identify how you make the motion.

- Clip slightly faster than you feel comfortable with (perhaps start the drill at the fourth bolt, so you are safe). Is there a particular draw/hand orientation that is harder? Practice on those. This is another way to ferret out problem areas.

- Most clip bobbles happen because you turn your attention to the next move before getting the rope 100% through. Your eyes moving to another target reflects this. On medium hard routes, force yourself one beat of focus more than normal when clipping. Watch the rope go all the way through the 'biner, wait a beat, then continue. Exaggerate it, so you lock your attention down on the target. Do this on routes where you feel semi-stressed as a way to burn this skill in when you are ready.

- A common reason for bobbles is bumping a draw that is dangling in space, causing it to sway or spin, creating a moving target. This typically occurs on overhanging terrain. Climb an easy route that has draws dangling in space. Do the basic clipping drill, taking mental note of any positions where you bobble. Climb the route again, slowing down that problem clip even more than you did the last time. If this route is difficult to you, rest one bolt before the problematic clip so you can fully focus on that problematic orientation. Concentrating on keeping your core tight can help a lot with stabilizing yourself while you cleanly clip the draw.

- On easy routes in safe positions, practice cross clipping with a lower or higher body to bolt orientation. So if you are holding on to a jug with your left hand, a cross-clip is with your right hand on the left side of your left hand. In this example, you might find it difficult to clip when the gate is facing the right, and the draw is on the wall, as opposed to dangling in space (i.e., less than or equal to vertical).

- As you continue to become more aware of the mechanics of clipping, breaking it down into the sub-movements, take stock of any other parts in the clipping motion outside of what I've mentioned. Are you finding other subtle aspects of this mechanic to which you could apply these mindful techniques?

- Have your belayer watch your clips, noting any issues. When you come down, debrief. How do you think you did? How did your belayer think you did?

- If you have trouble with a hand and gate position, then get yourself in place on an easy route and do as many of those as possible.

- Consider verbalizing the gate orientation, and the hand used to clip. Say "left clip, left hand" or whatever it is that will make sense to you to take note of the clip and your technique.

- If you have real trouble with a particular clip orientation, drag a rope on top-rope, mock-leading. Practice that clip orientation as much as possible up the route.

**Additional Gaze Drills:**

1. On a route of medium difficulty that you have ascended previously, find a stance mid-route where you can practice the *wide* gaze. Allow your conscious mind to turn off as you turn your eyes upwards on the route past the next couple of moves. Allow your subconscious to lead you to discoveries such as holds you've never seen or potential improvements of sequences you hadn't considered. If one pops into consciousness, then become more actively engaged with how to use it to your advantage.

2. On an easy top-rope, find a comfortable stance and gently close your eyes and relax. This may feel a bit uncomfortable to start with as we strongly associate sight with control. It may take a few routes practicing this before you feel relaxed enough with your eyes closed to notice how much more aware you become of your inner self. As you start to gain this awareness, scan around in your body, taking stock of how you feel physically.

3. Extend the previous drill by engaging the pinpoint gaze immediately after opening your eyes. Practice the quick transition from the relaxed inner focus of the off gaze to the decisiveness of the pinpoint gaze. As you open your eyes, pinpoint your next foothold.

4. Link a number of pinpoint gazes in a row, with particular intention focused on your feet.

5. After you climb a route, reflect back on how well you used your eyes. Were you conscious about matching your gaze to the situation?

# Chapter 3 - Breathing

We discussed one of the two meta-skills in the previous chapter with the examination of the use of our eyes to deploy attention and awareness. Let's now look at the other: breath control. The two meta-skills, the gaze and breath, form the bedrock of climbing craftsmanship. Using the breath skills outlined here both relaxes and empowers our ascents. The mindful application of the breath serves an orchestration role in conjunction with the gaze. Breathing well at once disperses stress while prodding us onwards. It's often the critical difference between a quality and a bungled ascent. Breathing well connotes climbing well. Moreover, a "well-breathed" climb is both more rewarding and more pleasant.

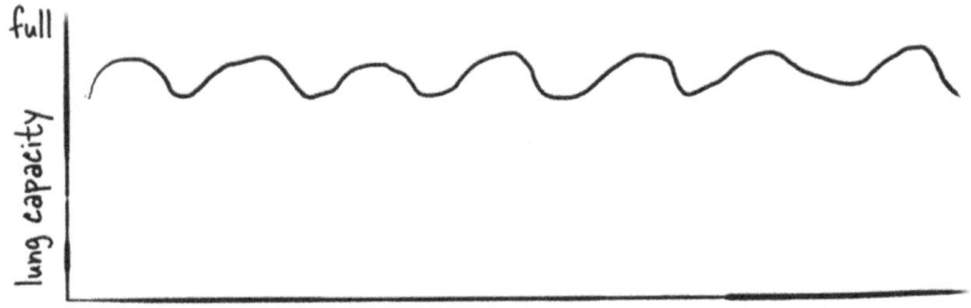


High frequency breathing from the chest reflects and creates tension

The benefits of skillful breathing are manifold. The breath helps disperse anxiety while climbing, helping distract from pump. Additionally, it decreases hesitating and freezing. It diminishes inner mental chatter while reducing negative thoughts. Your body tends to follow your breath. It links your consciousness and subconsciousness. It at once *associates* (makes you more attentive) and *dissociates* (makes you more aware and autonomic). The autonomic aspect helps you keep moving--becoming more a *doing* creature instead of a *thinking* one. Where holding your breath, or shallow, panting breathing, tends to freeze your body and mind, mindfully breathing acts as a lubricant, sliding you onward. Perhaps the most important blessing the breath confers is a sense of alert tranquility. Your mind at once sharpens and mellows through proficient breathing.

Much like an automotive engine flywheel carries inertial force, smoothing the motor to a purr, so too the bellows action of the lungs acts on the body. When a flywheel starts spinning, its inertia actuates the other engine components linked to it such as the pistons and crankshaft. The engine then "wants" to continue to run purely through the momentum of the flywheel. Our breath behaves similarly: as we inhale and exhale, the rest of our body tends to kinesthetically follow suit—a trait we may use to advantage while climbing. The breath, employed well, acts as a kind of auto-pilot for movement. Much like marshaling our eyes initiates action, the breath also subconsciously prods the body forward.

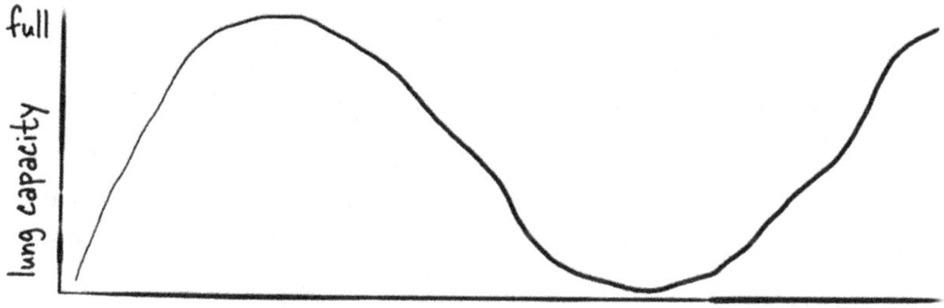


Deep, full breaths through belly disperses stress while clarifing focus

The breath operates both through conscious and unconscious control. While you won't ever totally forget to breathe while climbing, of course, the ideal patterns discussed in this chapter aren't likely your autonomic default: it takes proficiency to breath *well.* Without some training and conscious work, it's unlikely that your breath will end up aiding you as much as if you practice the sorts of techniques to follow. Unfortunately, the ideal breathing patterns aren't a totally fire-and-forget setting in your body. They require practice and focused attention.

With the many demands and stresses common in climbing—the strains of concentration and maximal muscular contractions—we might quickly lose track of breathing skillfully. Just about any challenging activity runs the risk of causing you to lose track of the breath, disrupting breathing from the full, deep patterns that aid power and tranquility. Since the breath doesn't require active control, once the ideal rhythm fades, the sharp demands of climbing drown out focus on the empowering breath, returning you to your less than perfect baseline.

With this loss, you may lose not only the beneficial aspects of well-executed breathing but also fall victim to the negatives of poor breath control. Where skillful breathing frees the mind and body in a virtuous cycle, the out-of-control, harried, shallow, and panting breathing patterns of a stressed or near-panic-stricken climber, or breaths unconsciously held out of angst, spins a vicious cycle, seizing the engine up. Through practice, you strengthen the natural association between the breath and movement such that even when you encounter moments of high physical stress or anxiety, the cadence of the breath continues to assist you. It takes dedicated practice and time to reinforce this bridge.

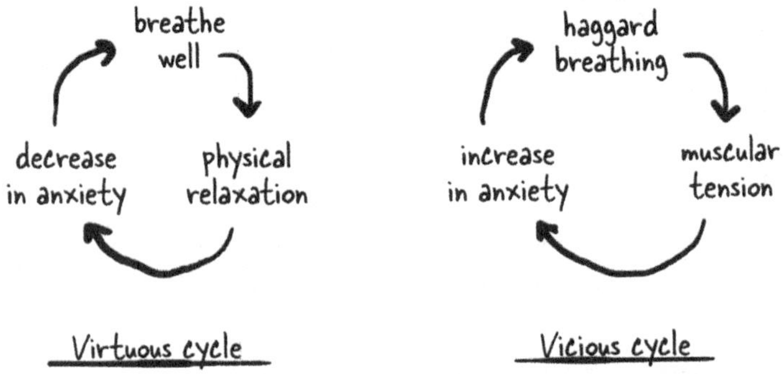


Effectively harnessing the breath is perhaps the most subtle and elusive of skills. Breathing well while ascending is nearly synonymous with skillful climbing. The two are intimately linked. Of all the skills in the book, this may be the most important. However, its benefit is mirrored both by its subtlety and its difficulty. More than the other skills presented here, improving breath control is difficult to relate through words. It's an exceedingly personal and introspective skill. Expect to revisit this chapter, mull the material over, and use yourself as an experimental subject over the long haul to see pervasive improvements in your breathing. Luckily, this practice mixes well with all sorts of activities, directly climbing related or not. It doesn't take the kind of exclusive dedication as, say, campusing to reap benefits. You can and should mix breath practice in with most of your climbing routines.

Practicing breathing while climbing is a particular challenge. In **Chapter 7**, we talk in detail about the need to practice at the correct level. With breathing, this is doubly important. While the restorative breath is comparatively easy to practice, conversely, the assertive power exhales present difficulties. On easy routes these seem artificial without the immediacy and prompting that arises from mental and physical challenge. However, as with the other skills we discuss in this book, practice is the only way to ensure skills like harnessing the breath remain available to us in times of stress. You can't just read this text and then expect to start power breathing effectively the next time you find yourself stressed on a hard on-sight.

Many drills presented in this book, such as clipping, work best when started on elementary routes for the climber. With breathing, however, it's harder to work the basics without enough stimulation. You want to find lines that are difficult enough to provoke *light* stress, but easy enough so that you can continue to focus on the breath, not the climbing. We want the breath to feel *needed*, but we also want a clear head to focus on the drill: we want to be *stressed*, but not *stressed out* or filled with anxiety.

## Concentrate on the exhale

As you breathe, you subconsciously stimulate yourself to act, particularly on the *exhale*. Perhaps a low-level sub-mind, as it detects the bottoming out of your lungs, is called to action to move the muscles to get air *back into* your lungs as a survival trait. This parasympathetic, low-level reaction to the requirement of the body to move the lungs may, in turn, generalize from "move the lungs" to "move ." If you concentrate on the exhale, pushing a little more air out, it heightens this subconscious sense of the need to replenish it. Practice exhaling *just a bit* more than usual. This extra bit exhorts your subconscious to inhale while also stimulating the rest of the body to take action, like when depressing a spring then releasing the pressure upon it releases that potential energy all at once.

> The breath carries movement inertia. Link the bellows of the breath to the motions of your ascent.

This linkage originates from the muscles of the diaphragm, not from the intercostals in your chest. Your mind is directly affected by the muscle set with which you choose to breathe. Under stress, our body tends to breathe more with the chest muscles, which feeds back tension and weight to the mind. In contrast, pulling deep into the belly using the diaphragm calms the psyche. If we practice overriding the natural tendency to overuse the chest muscles when anxious or tired, our subconscious will learn to keep belly breathing. Therefore, it is essential to practice breathing in the most effective style continually, using only the gut. Over time, this style takes hold, becoming automatic.

### *Match the breath to the situation*

We consider two general breathing styles: the *restorative breath,* which replenishes our reserves while lowering arousal, and the *power breath,* which generally increases arousal. The two forms are differentiated in broad strokes by the length of the exhale, with restorative breaths employing much longer exhale time then the inhale leg.

The relaxing slow exhale, or *restorative* breath, the breath that we use to collect ourselves at a rest position, resets our body and mind. The exhale here is slow with just a hint of resistance while exhaling through slightly pursed lips. The breath comes out as a *whoooooo.* This sound reflects your body and mind letting go of anxiety and muscular tensions, like air escaping a half-filled bag. Conversely, the assertive power breath exhales acts more forcefully like a bellows. It pushes us forward, providing cadence, diffusing thought while calling us to work. It's sometimes sharp and quick, like a punch, a Bruce Lee *chaaaaa!*

Often you use a restorative breath at a rest stance to re-charge, then a power breath through the hardest moves on a route. But sometimes the crux sequence requires the relaxation breath instead. This relaxation prepares you, for example, for an intricate technical sequence some distance above pro.

## Breathing Styles

Let's now turn our attention to specific ways to use the breath. In this chapter, we explore two categories, the restorative and the power breath, yet these are rather coarsely grained depictions of what is a very nuanced phenomenon. In reality, it's much more of a continuum. The description provided here simplifies this phenomenon to clarify the explanation.

The first category functions to restore and relax. The second encompasses ways of breathing to empower and disperse stress. This category is subdivided in two as well, giving a total of three breathing styles: one restorative and two empowering.

> Use a slow breath at rest stances to relax you body and restore your psyche. Use a power exhale to charge up, preparing for and reinforcing a more aggressive approach.

1. **Whoo:** the *restorative* breath is a slow exhale that drains away stress and anxiety from our body and mind, lowering our arousal. The exhale leg of the breath is significantly longer than the inhale.

2. **Wha:** a flowing *power* breath that forms the lion's share of our breathing while climbing. It stands in the middle ground between attention and awareness, keeping us at a medium state of arousal. The inhale and exhale legs are close to the same duration.

3. **Cha**: the other sort of empowering breath, used in situations where we need to generate full output. It's an *explosive* breath. The inhale is quick and deep, and then the breath is held until we explode it all out.

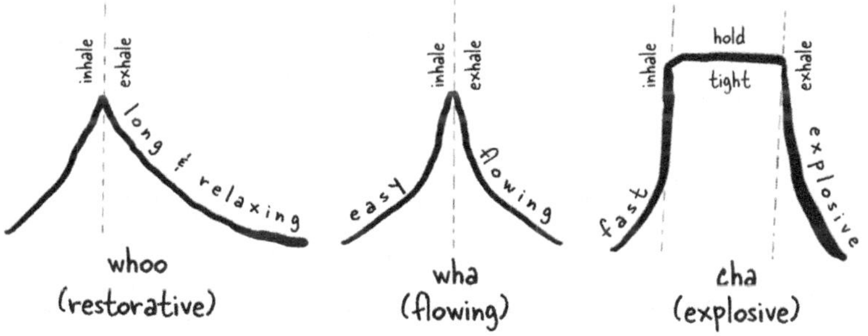


Let's now investigate each of these breaths in turn to see in what scenarios we want to use each, and how they help our climbing. The first sort, the *whoo*, is the primary tool we have to ease anxiety and dissipate physical and mental stress.

## The restorative breath (whoo)

The first sort of breathing we investigate, the *restorative* breath, helps recharge our physical and mental batteries. It is the primary skill we employ to regenerate energy and calm the rattled or exhausted psyche while climbing. It's one of the critical helpers in intra-route recovery. While we introduce the *whoo* here, we detail it further in the next chapter that explores restoration techniques, as we typically package restorative breathing along with other skills when resting.

With the relaxing slow breath, we shed muscular tensions and aggregated mental burdens intra-route. To get the most out of this restoration, breathe into your abdomen, activating the parasympathetic system: "belly breathing." Envision pulling a syringe: the plunger comes straight down, sucking in from the top—it doesn't expand outwards. Concentrate on the exhales, letting the inhales happen automatically. When exhaling, slightly purse your lips, so that you make a "whooo" (or similar) sound on exhale. This slight back pressure provides a specific sort of message to the brain. It appears that this back pressure caused by slight resistance on the exhale signals the parasympathetic system in a way that slows and calms the mind.

Let's investigate what it feels like to use the relaxation breath now as you read this. Either read the following first then practice, or, ideally, have someone read the following to you:

> Get comfortable sitting upright in a chair. Close your eyes slowly. Take a deep inhale in through your mouth down into your belly, pausing briefly at the natural top of the inhale. Slowly exhale through your mouth, feeling the tension in your body relax. Pause briefly again at the end of your exhale, then allow yourself to inhale naturally through your mouth back down into your stomach. On the next exhale, notice yourself relax even more. Feel your shoulders and neck let go. Inhale again into your belly. On this third exhale, imagine any remaining tension melting off of you. Continue this imagery, feeling your body relax for another three full breath cycles. At the end of the last exhale, slowly open your eyes. Take note of your sense of calm as your eyes open.

Hopefully, when you completed this example practice above, you found yourself with a greater sense of calm and clearer focus than when you began. You want to incorporate this sense of relaxation and regenerated reserve during your ascents, where appropriate.

The restorative breath slides us to awareness

You can practice this de-stressing activity above throughout your typical day-to-day life, helping your climbing. The more automatic you can make your reaction to stress in general, the more likely you will activate this restoration breathing when you need it while climbing. Ideally, we want to dump the bucket of accumulated anxiety as soon as we have the opportunity. Practicing this as part of your routine outside of climbing helps build this reflex into your subconscious. For example, if you find yourself waiting in an interminable line at the store when you are in a hurry, close your eyes and run through this three-breath de-stressing exercise.

## *Power breaths*

Now we turn focus to the second category of breathing, the *power breath*. Where the *restorative* breath chills us out, raising awareness of our inner self, the *power breath* orients our compass to the opposite pole. It deepens both focused attention and increased kinesthetic arousal to the external environment. Both breath types, relaxing and empowering, are essential. However, of the two, power breaths are used more frequently. We consider two sorts of power breaths in this chapter. The first sort is the fluid, relaxed belly breathing which we turn our attention to next. This type of breath serves to at once add to our power and distract us from the unhelpful ruminations of the mind, keeping us moving fluidly.

While moving, we usually want intense arousal to ascend quickly and decisively. The power breath buttresses this psychological state. The directed exhale, originating from the diaphragm and exiting the mouth, simultaneously locks in our attention while also settling our awareness. It acts as a self-regulator, helping set the internal slider bar to the correct level between these two forces of consciousness.

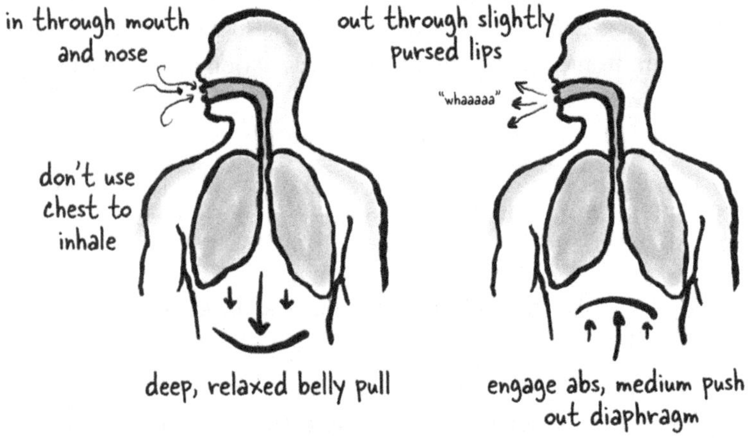


The "wha" breath keeps us fluid, relaxed, and moving

We often blend the skills of the gaze from the last chapter with the breath, choosing the best combination of eye and breath mechanics for a given situation. For example, deploying a pinpoint gaze to, say, laser in a foot micro-edge, heightens attention. Typically, choosing a fluid power exhale is an excellent choice to pair with the pinpoint gaze. It moderates laser focus so we don't get too locked in, leaving some awareness on the margin. This breath works synergistically with the gaze: it both underscores the attentive focus from the eyes while simultaneously mellowing its harsh edges.

## *Power Breath: wha*

Consider the first sort of power breath, the *wha*. Note, the actual sound may vary: a "hhhhhaaaaaaaaaa" may be more your taste, or something more exotic. Many sounds you could make while conforming to the steps to follow work, though you want to look out for exhales that sound tension-filled like a hissy "heeeea." Sound like this suggest the mouth pulled tight in a grimace, baring teeth. It's likely this sound originates from a taught neck and face. The sounds you make on exhale reflect the muscular tension of your face and neck. Keep the sound fluid and flowing as you climb, listening to yourself to ensure the breath stays that way. If it sounds tense, it likely results from muscular contraction above your shoulders, which in turn reflects your mental state.

The goal with the *wha* is to disperse tension while keeping the level of arousal high. The resulting sound, therefore, should sound fluid and relaxed. If you hear yourself sounding tense as you ascend, take action on your next breath to sound relaxed, deep, and full. To make the sound thus, your body must act accordingly, resulting in an actual release. In a virtuous cycle, this relaxation feeds back to your psyche, moderating anxiety.

Try these steps demonstrating the *wha* breath, just as you sit reading:

1. Take an inhale at normal speed in through your mouth down into your diaphragm ("belly breathing").

2. Allow the natural pause at the bottom of the breath cycle.

3. Force the breath out through your mouth by pushing slightly with your abdomen, slightly pursing your lips. Your cheeks should bulge out a bit as the constriction of your lips. Push out to where you notice the bottoming out of air, but don't create a vacuum in your chest. The sound is full, flowing, and powerful.

4. Allow the inhale to happen on its own, but grant a little intention to pushing the exhale. Focus just a bit on *emptying* the lungs.

Keep your breaths deep into your belly, not panting and short. The deep pull into your diaphragm reflects a deep reserve of power. If you are standing or seated upright, you should exhale hard enough to tilt very slightly inward from your core tension. However, *everything else should be very relaxed, particularly your face and neck.* As you exhale, your cheeks and lips, even while slightly pursed, should be relaxed enough that the force of the exhale balloons your cheeks outwards at the start of the exhale. The exhale then moves forward through your mouth, expanding your lips away from your gums by the end of the breath.

## *The wha breath is a power source*

The *wha* breath acts like wind to our sails. We give a slight restriction at our mouth to cause a small bit of back pressure, but the general feel of the breath is free and flowing. This mirrors how we want our body to behave as we ascend: relaxed and at ease. The *wha* breath is remarkable for its capacity to at once empower and relax. As such, it forms the foundation of power exhales: it's the primary way of breathing while climbing.

The "wha" breath floats between awareness & attention

Moreover, the *wha* exhale is an excellent way to set a cadence for ourselves during a multi-move sequence, like when we move between the perceived safety of a clipped piece of pro or bolt and the next chance for protection. It is the foundation for our internal metronome, the beat of which propels us upwards. Our body takes exhales as a cue to move. Thus, this sort of breathing is particularly helpful for climbers who tend to hang around too long or climb tentatively. Focus on following the cue of the exhale by executing your move at that moment.

You can get a feel for the cadence of the *wha* when out hiking, like on the approach to the crag, assuming it's strenuous enough for you to have some difficulty talking while walking. Or, the next time you walk several flights of stairs, allow yourself to settle into a rhythmic pattern of *wha* breathing as outlined. When engaged in a low-stress activity such as a hike or stair-climbing, it's easier then climbing to focus on how the exhale *wha* serves as a metronome of energy exchange. As you walk, focus attention on your diaphragm, feeling it plunge on the inhale, then intentionally give the exhale just a little juice. Concentrate on the brightening aspects of this way of breathing as it keeps you fluid and moving, your limbs merging in lock-step with your exhale. See if you can detect the slightly pleasant feel of the passage of air in and out of your body. This is the sort of assistance we want from our breath while climbing.

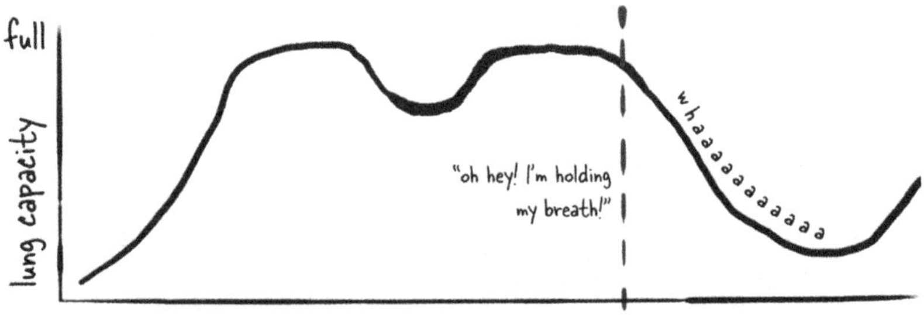


If you catch yourself holding your breath like this, engage in a wha.

In summary, the *wha* breath forms the basis of air exchange while climbing, and constitutes the majority of exhalations. Deep, full, and powerful, this breathing style at once sets the stage and urges us forward like a benevolent teammate or soothing, supportive coach. Unrestricted belly breathing with slightly restricted exhales take time to develop to the point where they buttress you during your most intense moments. With conscious practice, you will find yourself buoyed by this saturated and energizing free passage of air in and out of your lungs more often during ascent.

Breathing in this fashion takes practice so that it bakes into your subconscious System 1 routine. One way to help prime the pump is to consciously start the flow at the beginning of the route, just as you pull up onto the stone. Developing a standard practice of perhaps a calming *whoo* as you approach the route, then an empowering *wha* breath as you pull the first move signals to your locomotive to begin linking the breath cycles to your movement. This begins the chain of flowing assistive breaths continuing the entire line.

## Power breath: cha

Where the *wha* is all about the free flow of air to keep us loose and flowing, the *cha* uses the tension of the air in your lungs as a charge. It's as if the inhale tops off our battery for maximum output. We fill our lungs with this power, holding it ***momentarily*** until we fire off this charge with the "chaaaaaa" exhale, where we then fully release the tension we stored to maximize energy for that short period. Again, like the *wha*, the noise you make might be something quite different. Perhaps yours comes out more like a "pfhhhhh." If you are following these steps, consider it a *cha*:

1. Like the *wha*, inhale deeply with the diaphragm, but now inhale just a bit more air to fill the lungs, right where the top of your chest at your heart level starts to feel tight.

2. Hold the breath tightly to remain rigid through the core.

3. Make the move (or moves).

4. Wholly and quickly release the held energy, pushing out through the diaphragm. This will naturally come out sounding something like "chhhhaaaa!" On some moves, you exhale while moving, some you exhale after locking down the target hold.

The difference between the *wha* and *cha* is that the *wha* never stops the airflow. It's a free, unhindered (except for that slight back-pressure of the semi-pursed lips), and flowing. The *cha*, in contrast, pulls in a bit more air (there's some intention on the inhale), locks it off tight, moves, then explodes it all out.

Here's an example to make the purpose of the *cha* more concrete. Mentally envision yourself on a route of crimps where you see the next move—an obvious long reach to a small hold, requiring you to high step your right foot using your good current hand-holds, then explosively reaching up to that crimper with your right hand. When you hit the crimp, it will take a moment of struggling with it while your power bears down and you settle onto the hold. You need to hold this power, body tension, and concentration for a few seconds. This is where the *cha* breath comes to play. Holding the breath mirrors remaining high on the power curve for that couple of seconds while you work to initiate the move, then settle onto the target. In this example, after you feel positively engaged on the target, you explode the breath out.

The "cha" breath invokes attention

It's likely that under the duress of the problematic move, your face will tense up, filled with effort. Don't resist that momentary registration of stress in your face, but as soon as the *cha* comes out, allow your face and neck to relax by exploding the exhale out: *cha*! Don't continue to carry the tension afterword. The *cha* is a momentary spike in pressure, followed by complete release, resuming full belly breathing. It's a specialized version of *wha* where you hold your breath and keep your mental energy focused until a high-wattage move is complete.

You might want to try this out on an easy route to get a sense of what this breath pattern entails. You likely engage it from time to time without really registering its fine details. Here's one way on an easy gym route to get a sense of how the *cha* power breath works: locate a move where you skip a few holds to a long extension. As you dip down to semi-dynamically reach out for the target, begin the *cha* breath. Keep the air locked tight in your

# The Explosive "Cha" Breath

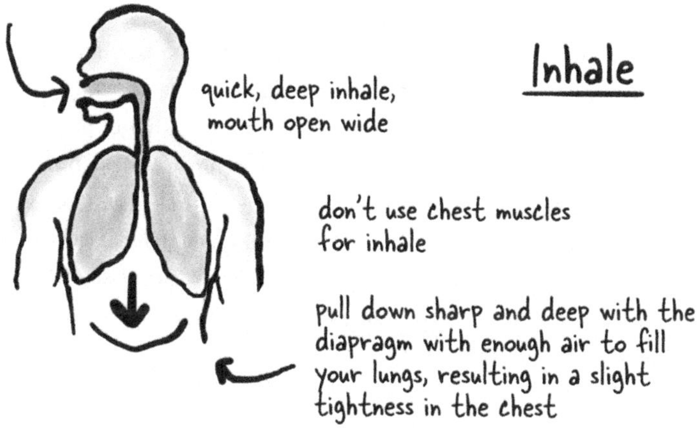


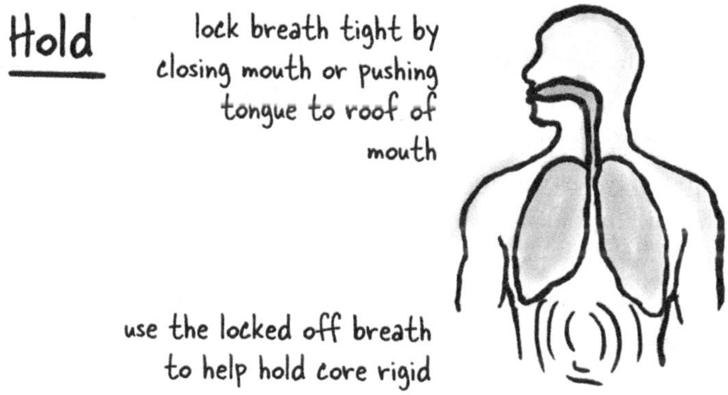


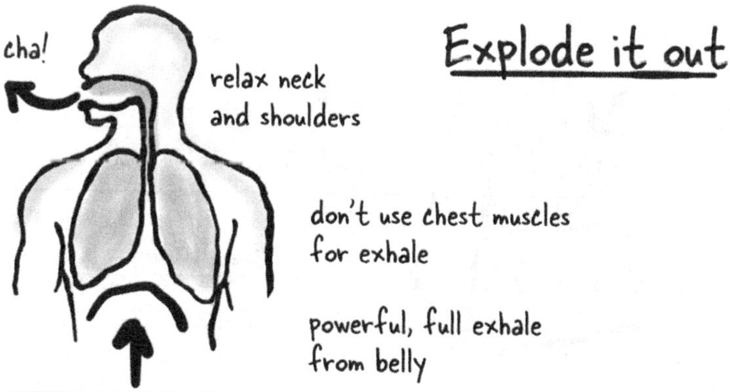

rigid core as you reach up to that distant target. When you hit it, let yourself settle onto the target. As soon as you feel comfortable on it, release all of that pent-up pressure in a *cha!* Notice how the body tension and rigidity of your core bolster your power.

Sometimes, with powerful multi-move sequences, you will modify the *cha* breath slightly. Say we extend our previous example so it has another difficult move: a long pull to a decent but exacting three-finger pocket. You want the power and body tension of the first move *cha*, but you can't let it all out when you hit the first hold like before. In cases like this, you don't fully release your tension upon managing the first hold. You instead *cha* out half of the reserve then quickly inhale to full lung capacity for the stretch to the three finger pocket. You then complete the *cha,* releasing the residual tension, and bottoming out your lungs.

## Breath cadence

Both sorts of power breaths, the *wha* and *cha*, act as ticks of the metronome, keeping your body moving, your intuition high, and your brain in check. More than that, engaging in this kind of power breathing recharges your battery of reserve power and makes each move more punchy. Over time, you may start to intuit a sense of the energy associated with the breath. Holding it in and remaining tight with your chest as a result of a *cha* breath mimics the necessity of keeping the high intensity and full-body tension that the move requires. As soon as your body adapts to that hold, you immediately release that tension with the *cha* to allow yourself to recharge.

The breath keeps the body ascending, giving our moves more punch

Those in the combative sports such as boxing or MMA use their breath somewhat similarly, changing their breathing style to match the moment. Watch a boxing match with your attention focused on how the combatants breathe. You may notice how they tailor their breathing to the demands of the situation. For example, they exhale sharply while punching. It's almost like the breath acts as a catalyst for the hands. We want to mimic this while climbing, harnessing the explosiveness of the exhale to propel us upwards. Each inhale replenishes the battery. Each exhale uses that power to both physically ascend and stay mentally fluid. Most of the time while climbing, you engage in one of the breathing techniques discussed in this chapter. Like a locomotive, if you don't connect the cars of the different breath cycles, the power will not transmit down the line. Keep each breath cycle fastened one after the other with few to any gaps.

No two breaths are identical, yet some patterns emerge that help energize or restore you while climbing. Those discussed here, while applicable to most scenarios, certainly do not cover all of the different subtle ways of deploying the breath you might identify. It's likely as you become more aware of your breathing during climbing that you stumble upon new specialty alternatives. By listening to yourself and by observing others who breathe well, I suspect you may find new patterns of breathing to add to your arsenal.

A tricky thing about harnessing the breath is that it's possible to mimic a facsimile of the energizing breaths described here, but the actual result ends up reinforcing the wrong things. Some climbers huff and puff like dragons, but the impact of this on their climbing ends up just bluster to little effect. There's no flow, no release of tension: it sounds quite the opposite, and their climbing shows it. Their breath mirrors their internal psyche: blocked up, filled with tension. Their breath loops feedback of these feelings to their detriment. Big booming breaths don't necessarily equate assistance to your ascent, sometimes, exactly the converse.

Observing skilled breathers is difficult as there aren't many exemplars. If you are fortunate enough to know one in real life, make a study of him or her. Otherwise, look up videos[1] of Adam Ondra to observe a master breather. And, for bonus credit, watch it once, then replay it, but that time, just *listen.*

# On Screaming!

Climbing can be very lonely, all by yourself up there. While under the physical stress, the emotional turmoil, and fear-inducing terrain so prevalent in this sport, any little thing you can do to support yourself helps. The breath takes on a slightly depersonalized aspect when used well. It almost stands apart from you, acting as a benevolent bystander, whispering soothing affirmations your way. Vocalizing with the exhale, letting out grunts and yells raises this a notch. The invisible accomplice of your voice asserts: "Do it!" In a virtuous feedback cycle, as you yell out in exhale, you also hear this aggression, fueling us upwards. Vocalizing feeds back additional power to your psyche.

For some, the thought of the noisy power-exhales doesn't fit their self-image: only meatheads or jocks would be so gauche as to be so loud with their breath and voice when climbing. They feel self-conscious like they would be drawing attention to themselves with the exhales, particularly when they feel unsure or stressed.

While this attitude is understandable, the tool of loud exhales and screams are as crucial in ascent as others. It is particularly helpful at unsticking us when we hit a moment of uncertainty. A yell right at the momentary pause when we feel ready to give up can defrost us to *make the freaking move already.* Climbers who tend to freeze at the critical moment should practice yelling out, right when the thought of saying "take" enters the mind. Convert the thought of "take" to an external scream. Your body will follow suit by moving. It's remarkable how much screaming combats inner resistance, providing an immediate antidote to paralysis. If you tend to stall out and are not yelling, grunting, or otherwise vocalizing, screaming can serve as a corrective. When you hear the inner voice saying "no," respond (assuming the environment is safe) with a scream.

---

[1] *search "Ondra La Dura Dura" for a good example.*

Vocalizations take all sorts of forms, from barely audible squeaks to banshee screams from the depths of hell. Of the various kinds, it's the high decibel outputs that are perhaps the most helpful as these mega-wattage outbursts often spell the difference between successfully giving it your all and whimpering "take" instead. If you are encountering high doubt, produce maximum decibels in response.

- Like the *cha*, your voice should be truly explosive. Use the energy of the exhale. Imagine that you are harvesting the energy from a TNT blast.

- Screaming is about giving it everything and holding back nothing, which is typically not very pretty. Stay humble, sincere, and raw.

- The moments that require a scream often stand at the threshold where success is about fifty-fifty: you may not be up to the task. The scream says "I may not have enough for this move, but I'm giving everything, letting the cards land where they may." Keep this script close at hand.

- Don't stop the force of air at the end (if you have a choice). Let it die out with the remainder of the breath. We don't want any of that energy remaining as residual tension. Screaming is about letting go. You can reflect this intention by keeping air moving through your breath cycle without a hitch.

- Screaming is for *you*. Beware of your ego. Some people scream for *others*, as a kind of ego pronouncement. Some suppress screams out of ego management in reverse: they *don't* scream because of others.

# Chapter Three Summary

**Your breath enlivens and restores you. Keep regularly breathing through your belly to stay moving fluidly and relaxed.**

In this chapter, we detailed three primary breath tools:

1. The restorative **whoo** breath helps disperse tension, recharging the mind and body.

2. Using the **wha** power breath facilitates unrestricted, free-flowing, movement. Using our belly as a set of bellows, we set a cadence to our ascent.

3. Deploying the **cha**: this breath uses the *momentary* tension of the held breath with full lungs for maximum engagement. Using the release of that brief tension in the "cha" exhale out of our mouth propels us back into a flowing, relaxing movement cycle.

Harnessing the breath is a vast topic worthy of study. In this chapter, I've described a few techniques—likely plenty to incorporate and practice. Most climbers don't employ much skill with the breath, so growing conversant with these is a great way to start.

- Breathing grants cadence, keeping you moving.
- Breathing can get you out of the mind and into the body.
- Slow, relaxed belly breathing can restore and calm you.
- "Power" exhales can rev you up and get you moving purposely
- The breath facilitates movement inertia.
- Your voice can empower you. Practice ways of harnessing its unique way of "un-sticking" your trouble spots.

## *Whoo: restorative breath*

| Helps Facilitate | Use When |
|---|---|
| • physical recovery<br>• mental restoration<br>• introspection | • at rests<br>• easy moves |

## *Wha: flowing breath*

| Helps Facilitate | Use When |
|---|---|
| • unrestricted movement<br>• dispersing stress<br>• moderate attention | • not using another breath<br>• feeling anxiety, stress<br>• Resuming climbing after a rest |

## *Cha: explosive breath*

| Helps Facilitate | Use When |
|---|---|
| • intense focus<br>• body tension<br>• maximal output | • big moves<br>• deadpoints<br>• dynos<br>• cruxes |

During easy climbing like your warm-ups, focus on full, relaxing *whoo* breaths. Tell your belayer, if applicable, of your intent. At the bottom of the route, prime the pump: close your eyes, taking three deep, relaxing breaths, feeling any tension in your body leave on the exhale. Open your eyes, take in a deep breath, then exhale strongly using the "power exhale" technique as you make the first move.

Continue up the route, maintaining an awareness of your breath. If you note that you have wavered from the *wha/cha* breath, then slow your climbing down, turning your attention more to the breath for a move or two to get it back on track. Feel the sense of fluidity in a move linked with an exhale.

- At rest stances, practice the *whoo*, taking as many restorative exhales as the stance allows.

- When you make the next move from this rest stance, powerfully exhale using the *wha* breath as you reach for the hold. Notice how the breath empowers your movement.

Practice this drill regularly during your warm-ups. Consider more advanced drills after you master the basics:

1. **Power breath at the crux**. Find a route with a hard but doable crux. Rest on the rope below this crux. While resting, visualize the move to come, envisioning your breath as part of this sequence. After the rest, when you take your body weight back, start moving again after a powerful *wha/cha* as a way to practice harnessing the empowering breath during this sequence.

2. **Consistent Breathing**. On a route that is hard for you, but well within your ability level, practice breathing the entire route. Engage this climb in practice mode, meaning that success on the route is how well you accomplish your breathing goal. Completing the route cleanly is not important. The goal is to breathe well.

3. **Breathing when it counts**. Choose a line that is hard for you. If you feel a sense of fear either of falling or of failure, immediately exhale strongly with the *wha* breath and make a move. Success or failure is dictated by how well you remember to act this breathing mechanic, not if it results in you completing the move. We want to practice learning to respond to stress through the

breath—it can take a while to remember to do so when we are captured by stress. Holding the breath reflects stress. We want to practice breaking this tendency.

4. On harder routes, **explore vocalizing**. Let it rip, particularly if you don't often grunt or squeal in effort. These screams are a way of letting go of tension and resistance. Take note of how this works as you scream.

5. The **cha breath** takes a little bit of practice to get a feel for, then some work to find the places to best employ it. Use easy warm-up routes to find places where it's easy to skip holds so you practice this important breathing technique of holding your breath to engage the core, then fully releasing it. A good *cha* breath does not keep any residual tension after it's complete.

6. **Explore the difference between the wha and cha breaths**. The *wha* does not fully impede the flow of air, where the *cha* blocks it at the top of a strong inhale to use this tension as an additional momentary boost of power, immediately releasing it.

7. **Reflect on breathing**. After each ascent, spend just a few moments reflecting back on how you breathed. Were you tight and congested? Loose and free? Were there any sequences that you breathed through particularly well or poorly?

# Chapter 4 - Restoration

Becoming proficient with the two meta-skills investigated in last two chapters—using the eyes and the breath—undergirds the craft of climbing. These meta-skills lie at the top of the tool chest, invocable regardless of the situation or difficulty. When in a spot of bother, the quick selection and deployment of one of these skills such as the pinpoint gaze or a *wha* breath helps bail you out.

Next, we build upon this base like the next level of stones in a pyramid. This next layer of foundational skills also plays a critical role in climbing, but, unlike the meta-skills, the aptitude we turn to next, inter-route restoration, isn't always available to us. Sometimes, as we all know, we would love to snatch a quick repose on route, but the climbing doesn't allow it. This chapter explores both finding ways to restore energy, and to then use those intra-route pauses to maximal effect. While we might not deploy the rest skills as often as the meta-skills, improving at these restorative proficiencies allows you to find and use them increasingly more often and more productively.

## *Tranquility*

Climbing physically and mentally relaxed imparts several benefits. Firstly, it promotes efficiency: you don't waste resources remaining tense, with muscles half-activated to no end. Secondly, it transforms the ascent into a more enjoyable, flowing one. Physical turgidity reflects and creates mental stress. Purposeless muscular tension is both the result and a cause of fear, apprehension, and anxiety. The skills in this chapter focus on ways to relax the body and mind. Climbing is often quite demanding and intense. Engaging in restoration skills actively discharges strains, resulting in more gas in the tank while increasing your sense of calm. The restoration skills presented here serve two purposes: they help recharge your batteries, and they help you maintain tranquility.

The term *tranquility* denotes a mind free from disturbance. Your psyche remains alert and clear. We aren't seeking somnolence or any sort of dull or sedated state of mind through the pursuit of tranquility while climbing, but, instead, ideally, a mind in perfect balance between attention and awareness. Climbing presents many objective stressors that wear us out. On our hardest ascents, we will certainly lose tranquility as we near exhaustion. The goal is to *delay* and *manage* the way the route drains these resources. We want only the *objective* stressors to strip our tranquility, not self-fabricated *subjective* ones.

Our psychological arousal level finds equilibrium between two competing forces, the sympathetic (revving) and the parasympathetic (calming) nervous systems. The two continuously vie for control. As one ascends in priority, we reap more benefits from its specialization at the cost of the other. Activities as strenuous as climbing lean heavily on the sympathetic avenue to render high wattage outputs. When we find opportunity to engage the parasympathetic, we want to do so as skillfully as possible so to reap as much relaxation as possible from this mode. This chapter explores techniques to that end.

Climbers almost never need more arousal while ascending. The physical and psychological forces in play during even the most simple climbs stomp hard—too hard, often—on the sympathetic accelerator pedal. While ascending, we nearly always need to keep a foot on the brake, activating the parasympathetic to keep a fresh mind and body. Almost always, the challenge for climbers is to moderate over-stimulation. In **Chapter 3**, we discussed how the breath helps us remain calm. We continue this line of reasoning in this chapter with additional techniques that foster a tranquil mind.

> Efficient climbing arises from tranquility.

We draw upon the meta-skills already presented, combining them to form two primary resting skills—the *rag doll*, and the *body scan*. By the judicious use of these two skills, we shed stress and anxiety while ascending, which helps us remain physically and mentally fresher than if we just plowed forward. With more gas in the tank, chances improve to conquer difficulties up-route. Armed with this presence of mind, we can better apply our muscles economically, instead of spastically wasting energy due to an exhausted psyche no longer able to regulate the effort.

While most commonly think of resting while climbing as a way to help the muscles, it's actually equally true that it's boon to the mind. Engaging in these restoration skills allows us to reestablish mental clarity, clearing out the cobwebs that form from the stress of ascent. With the mind in full command, it marshals the muscles decisively and makes clear, decisive tactical decisions.

## *Resting is only a rest when it's restful*

While the resting skills presented in this chapter are vital, we must also make a careful study of not overusing them. Resting is a function both of the biomechanical position (how good the rest stance is in general), and how "restful" it is for your level of fitness. Fitter climbers can rest for longer at a given position than weaker ones, their muscles remaining aerobic and well within capacity to restore energy. Elite climbers can effectively rest on the cruxes for us mere mortals. It's important to choose both the correct places to rest and the duration you stay there given your current fitness and rest skill ability. Additionally, sometimes, a seemingly excellent location to pause should be skipped entirely for various tactical reasons. Say, perhaps, you know an even better rest position is coming up in just three more moves, so you choose to skip the good but calf-burning stem, opting instead to punch it to the no-hands ledge.

"Rests" can also serve as a stalling tactic for tentative climbers who want to procrastinate out of fears such as the concern that they may not be good enough to do the next sequence. True rests charge us up. We don't want a "rest" to be another excuse to turtle, scurry onto the hamster wheel of anxiety, or otherwise waste energy. It's only really a rest if you recuperate either physically or mentally and it ultimately assists your ascent, else it's just an additional stressor and drain on energy. Rests are there to help us succeed in our goals, not an end in themselves. While most climbers under-utilize intra-route resting generally, it's not effective to simply invert this position. Instead, practice evaluating and judiciously deploying resting techniques only to the extent that they buttress efficient climbing.

Through practice, the surface area of effective resting grows. You get better at both finding and using intra-route pauses to restore energy. Practice the discovery and deployment of rests on easier routes so you can deploy both your increased wisdom to find rest positions and your physical technique to wring the most out of the stances you find. Learning the little details about how climbs grant repose and how to best use them is as vital a skill as any. As your aptitude increases, more positions you unearth climbing become truly restorative, and thus an overall benefit to the ascent.

# Rag Doll

Let's now turn to the first of two primary resting skills. When we get a break in the action while climbing, we can incorporate the restorative breath partnered with the *off* gaze in a powerful technique called the *rag doll.*

The rag doll technique is a way to mentally and physically recover while climbing, a sort of in-route nap. The primary skill in this regard is the restorative *whoo* breath. In the previous chapter, we practiced the restorative breath (**p. 50**) while sitting on the couch. Now we want to see how we can bring that same level of rest and calm to our ascents. In short, with the rag doll, you get as close to being asleep on the climb as possible without falling off. Just like a good night's sleep restores you for the next day, these little intra-route snoozes recharge the batteries for the challenges above.

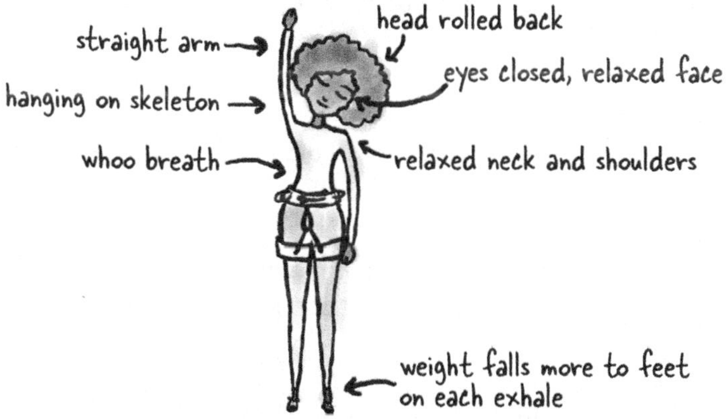


The rag doll hang: an intra-route nap

The rag doll helps restore your body and mind. One reason mental restoration occurs is because it's easier for the psyche to let go of the past and focus on the climbing above by breaking the route into sections. Instead of one big problem, you wrestle with a few smaller ones. These sections are marked by rest pauses, much like we split the stream of time into days by going to sleep at night. Deep rests grant a place where we can let go of the previous events on the route, allowing us to concentrate on what remains of the route as we proceed. As sleep denotes the end of the day and the start of another, we want intra-route rests to act as mental reset points, allowing our subconscious to drop past stresses and anxieties. The rag doll skill is a primary way of imitating the mentally restorative aspects of sleep on our psyche. When we mime sleep through the rag doll hang, we split the route into smaller, more digestible chunks.

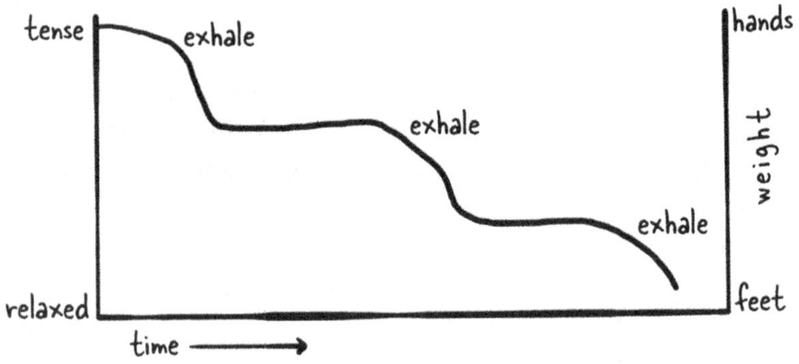


With each exhale, concentrate on the stress melting away

You can see in the image on the previous page how this technique gained its name: the climber literally hangs like a rag doll from one arm. Her body is limp as if she's asleep, just dangling there. This is the pose you want to mimic as much as the stance allows, so you rest fully. The image is an idealized rag doll pose; many other stances work as well. It's not the exact look you are after, it's the *result*. You could get a great rag doll in a no-hands kneebar, a well-balanced yet delicate face, or in a burly stem, just as examples.

While learning this technique, choose great stances with big holds so you can dangle like the climber in the illustration while also concentrating your attention on the rag doll skill, not the climbing.

1. Use the *off* gaze detailed in **Chapter 2.** Disengage your sight.

2. Engage in the restorative breath (the *whoo*) outlined in the previous chapter. With each exhale, feel the decrease in stress and muscular tension. Focus mainly on relaxing your neck, face, and shoulders, letting your head slump as if you were asleep.

3. On each exhale, feel the tension melt away and your weight fall more to your feet. Allow your neck to relax and even perhaps your head to roll back.

4. After three exhales, open your eyes. Take note of how you feel.

With conscious effort, you can improve the ability to recharge your batteries. Practice getting deep relaxation on easy routes so you can cultivate an inner sense of what the mental reset feels like—this deep, almost asleep restoration. The more you rehearse, the more likely you will use these skills effectively during your more intense climbs. With practice, efficient resting becomes second nature—you are more likely to remember to engage in rest and perform the aptitude well under times of stress. While this reduces the stress level on your body, it also reduces the cognitive load on your psyche.

# Body Scan

Learning to rest and relax efficiently is no accident: you practice ways of quickly assuming deep rest, and by this practice, get better at restoring your powers intra-route. Improving your ability to discern these retained tensions helps you identify areas in your body that you can relax further, a technique known as *body scanning*. This technique is a more active version of the rag doll. With the rag doll, you mostly want to disengage, tune out, and unwind. With the body scan you get specific, analyzing the state of distinct parts of your body. If you have, say, eight different places in your body under tension when at a resting stance, a quick body scan, where you inwardly pass downwards through your body looking for tensions, may reveal that some of them are superfluous. One muscle group is tense, but it could totally relax. It's holding taut out of some phantom need. Additionally, the scan may uncover other muscles working much harder than required to stay affixed to the wall. Relaxing those muscles so they work just enough—but no more—feeds back less stress to your psyche, allowing your mind additional recovery. Letting go of the physical burden in turn lightens your mental load.

As you learn how to deploy the body scan, find good stances so you can get comfortable enough to turn your attention inwards:

1. As you stand in a rag doll stance, using the *whoo* breath and the *off* gaze, scan down through your body just taking note of any areas of your body that feel overly tight. Match the exhale to your internal scan so you reach your feet at the end of your breath.

2. At the bottom of your exhale, start quickly reviewing those tight areas you found, continuing to do so as you naturally inhale. What muscles seem like they are working harder than they need to? Are there any that seem like they are unneeded? Choose the biggest offender. This is a snap judgment—pick the tight area you want to relax as you top off your inhale. There's no wrong answer.

3. On the next exhale, send your attention to that chosen tight area. Intend to release that tension in that group, matching the exhale of your breath to the strain of muscle, letting it go as your breath leaves your body. Try envisioning that muscle appearing as a balloon, deflating and softening, or consider it made of wax, melting and dripping away with your exhale.

4. Repeat these steps as long as you have remaining tensions and can comfortably stay in your rag doll stance.

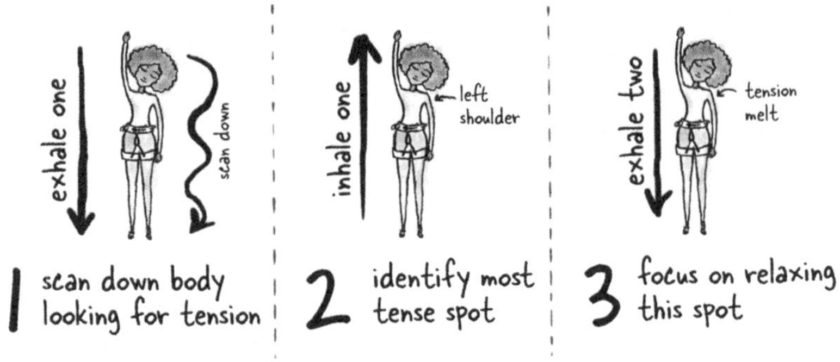


As you improve at the skill, practice applying aspects of the body scan technique at more marginal rest positions. Perhaps you get a stance only supporting one good restful exhale. Work to use the exhale in tandem with the body scan in one pass by exhaling while alert to any high tension spots. As soon as you hit one, use the rest of that exhale to disperse the tension from that spot.

With practice, you can apply the body scan to moments where the movements are easy enough that they don't demand full attention. With some of your consciousness therefore still available, you can, while moving, direct your attention to a part of your body, say your neck and upper back, scanning through them to ensure they are not retaining shadowy strains, even while they are under load. Linking the scan to the exhale reinforces the sense of release as the air leaving the lungs reflects the tension melting away from the hot spot you discovered.

With repetition, you might begin to find patterns or places where you tend to squirrel away stress and anxiety. Add this to an internal checklist to which you can quickly turn at small pauses. On smaller rests, like those of perhaps half a restorative exhale, you can just run through your checklist to see how these areas are managing, particularly if you tend to aggregate loads of tension. Clipping stances often have opportunities for quick rests, so you could make it a matter of routine to focus entirely on the clip, then take the "half restorative exhale," turning your attention immediately to your list of usual suspects. Say, for example, you know you tend not to relax completely onto your shoulder joint, but instead add a bit of unneeded muscular tension, pulling up slightly. You would clip, then with that quicker restorative exhale, send your attention to your shoulder to relax it entirely. Instead of looking for hot spots at these small rests, you pick a usual suspect and use the micro-repose to keep it loose and tension free.

Habitual hot spots we regularly uncover through the body scan are important to identify. Through returning to these trouble areas and working to keep them tension-free, we keep our energy high by not wasting it in dribs and drabs. This improved physical efficiency improves our psyche as well, for as we tire physically, we also tend to deplete our concentration.

When relaxing with the rag doll or body scan technique, we often don't know exactly how much we can release muscular tension without falling off. The closer we get to this line (within reason), the more stress and strain we can unload, granting us greater mental and physical reserves farther up the route. With each exhale, we can scan through the body looking for problem areas, using the feedback from our body to explore how much more we can relax. It's surprising how little it usually takes to remain on the wall, suggesting that by default, our "natural" sense of what force we need to stay affixed is pretty significant overkill for most stances, and likely climbing writ large. With each exhale while engaging in the rag doll or body scan, the muscles relax, and we pull less strenuously with the hands. It seems as if that newly established level is the minimum required to stay affixed, yet with each exhale, we relax further still.

# Relaxing Away Past Anxieties

With each obstacle we overcome in ascent, an imprint stamps on our mind, a kind of psychic weight or physical memory. These worries and anxieties we climb past often manifest in the body as muscular tensions, accumulating in an unseen slag heap. For example, say you move through a six-move crux sequence on tenuous slopers uncomfortably far from your last bolt. These moves take all of your concentration, ending at a precarious stance. Intense sequences such as this tend to leave your body with aggregated turgidity, the result of that crux stress. Your body preserves memory from the ordeal. In this way, it's actually the *body* that remembers the event, more than the mind.

> When you overcome stressors on a route such as a difficult section, an imprint of muscular tension remains. Clear this tension at the first opportunity via a rest skill.

Muscular tension depletes psychic energy. The sub-mind managing the muscular control of the tense groups grows weary; this drains your psyche, leaving your mind less capable of skillful direction of your intentions. You subconsciously carry those residual muscular tensions forward if you don't consciously work to let go of them, making the real and immediate climbing above more difficult than it really is. Your shoulders, neck, and deltoids may be pulling on the holds much harder than needed. If you don't make a conscious effort to let go of that accumulated stress, it will result in you pulling the next move itself and some residual weight of accumulated strains from past sequence as well. Without release at the moment, the psychological difficulties you struggled with get shunted to your body, where they fester until you do something about it. Scan for these anxieties manifesting as muscular tension, then actively work on relaxing them. This lets the past

Take advantage of micro-rests when they appear. For example:

As Maya pinpoints the deadpoint target, her stress level rises.

The moment she manages the hold, she immediately relaxes into a wha breath while using the off gaze. She feels tension leave her body and more of her weight transfer to her feet. She then resumes movement after this one second pause. This rest is so quick no one but her even knows it happened.

anxieties go so you don't continue carrying them onwards. The hidden haul bag you drag beneath you, slowly filling with debris, needs attention so it doesn't pull you down.

It's counter-intuitive to close your eyes when climbing, but this increase in consciousness into the inner state of the body. While climbing, so much consciousness comes from and is directed to the exterior world in general and our arms specifically. At appropriate stances, where we can employ the *off* gaze, we have a chance to explore through our body with this inwardly-directed focus, finding any of these squirreled away hot spots, using our attention inwards to let them go. Releasing the tensions of somatic memories frees mental resource. If we can identify these residual tensions in our body, actively letting them go, stress and anxiety dissipate from the mind. Relaxing the shoulders, for example, decreases fear of falling or failure. Suddenly, the climbing feels less difficult.

# Quick Rests

Rest positions come in all sorts of varieties, allowing for different depths of rest. As you become proficient at identifying how to quickly take advantage of the best rest positions where you can get multi-breath rag dolls or body scans, learning to take full use of what a given climb grants you in positions that are more marginal helps you retain and rejuvenate energy. These positions don't allow you to hang around forever in a rag doll, achieving complete recovery. Instead, these spots are just enough to slow the accumulation of mental and physical stress. With quick rests, you typically compromise, choosing to rest just one muscle group, such as your shoulders, or just relax your psyche for a second.

Feeling anxious, Maya takes a quick rest when she encounters a brief repose on the route. She closes her eyes, relaxes her face and neck, and lets out a single whoo exhale to rejuvenate her mind and shed stress before continuing.

Not all rests are going to be conducive to the deepest possible rag doll, but even brief pauses can give you some of the benefits of deep resting. Learning how to engage quickly and see the positive results from good rag dolls helps you identify and exploit more marginal stances. Often, for example, a clipping stance is good enough to clip, close the eyes, and give one deep relaxing *whoo* exhale before continuing. Learning to identify and maximize these opportunities translates into more focus and therefore more ability to unleash your physical power higher on the climb. There are a lot of little tricks and subtleties you can pick up if you look for them to get little rests here and there. Use the *off* gaze and the restorative breath as often as possible when you find them. Learn what it feels like to get into the deep recovery state through full multiple breath rag dolls so you have an internal barometer to measure the depth of rest.

Increase the stressful positions you rag doll and body scan in on practice ascents as your proficiency at these techniques improve as a way to help you regenerate energy at more marginal rest stances. Practice resting efficiently in a deep flag on overhanging terrain, for example. Or in a drop-knee position. During practice, you might not be as efficient in total on the route with all the rag dolling as you would be if you weren't as intent on getting those rests. This allows you to get better at this particular skill so you can use it to your advantage during performances you care about. Keep practicing. You improve at resting if you work at it, though it takes time like any other skill.

After you have a good sense of what that deep relaxation feels like, try shorter durations. Do one breath rag dolls and see how relaxed you can get. Try half a breath. After you get good at quickly transitioning to a rag doll, it's remarkable how much you can get out of a half-breath. These short rag dolls are a great skills in your arsenal, as these half-rests are much more common than full-blown three or more breath mega-rests. On shorter rag dolls, you might only really be able to close your eyes and exhale quickly without a deep hang. Take note of what you can get out of with just that. As you progress, you might incorporate these rest skills with actually moving—close your eyes, start the exhale and feel the relaxation drip begin, but then use that moment to slingshot yourself into the next move, for example. These techniques are subtle, requiring judicious application so as to add to your reserve, not draining it further.

> Think of quick rests as invisible moves that require attention and skill like any other.

Small, partial rests are the most frequently encountered ways of snatching rejuvenation in-route. Learning how to identify and exploit them grants the climber opportunity to substitute technique for strength. Sometimes, finding a few small rests here and there can spell the difference between success and failure. Taking full advantage of any quick rest you find helps further. As a case in point, consider a climber who found a knee scum to help a place a cam. Perhaps that incomplete kneebar is still good enough for a restorative breath exhale after completing the clip, but before making any more moves. Adding just this single exhale at this stance rejuvenates the mind and body, even if only by a small dose.

These micro-rests are a valuable tool to manage stress and fatigue because they occur with frequency on most all routes. Often, just the conscious turn to the intent to relax coupled with a *whoo* or *wha* exhale is enough for you to feel some tension dissipate. Executing a handful of these or more up the line adds up to a significant displacement of stress and tension, though it's likely undetectable to anyone but yourself, as these quick rests are often not discernible to others from actual movement.

> As a rule of thumb, employ rests lower on the route, then work faster and skip marginal rests at the end.

Make it part of your climbing routine to ferret out these quick rest stances. Perhaps in the gym, when you are repeating a route you know, you use the opportunity to hunt for them both by attempting to rest in novel ways yourself and by observing others climb it. Most climbers fail to look for and then utilize rest stances in general, and quick rests in particular. Finding them is as much of a skill as using them to best advantage. Less skillful climbers under-utilize rests opportunities low on a route, then attempt rests at locations towards the end as they tire, often resulting in compounding their problem. They don't have enough strength left to use even larger holds, so they end up stalling out and burning the remainder of their gas in a futile attempt to recharge.

## Exclusive Focus

With all the stimulus present while climbing, modulating away from vigilant movement to calm relaxation isn't trivial: it's hard to relax quickly and fully. Yet without conscious intent ceded to chilling out, recovery ends up sub-par.

It's a common malady for climbers to think they can effectively both rest and perform other skills at the same time, but, unfortunately, restoration mixes poorly with everything else when time is of the essence. If you try combining it with other skills, restoration becomes the distant secondary task, fading sub-effectually to the background while you, say, chalk up. You get the most out of rest positions by clear, unadulterated concentration on *just resting*. This is accomplished by focusing fully on the resting skill instead of attempting to mix the rest with other tasks such as planning moves or futzing with your harness.

If you want to use a ten second stance to both rearrange some cams while also recovering, for example, know that your recovery is far from ideal during that pause. Sometimes, the dual-purposing of this ten seconds is worth it, but there's a devil's bargain: your rest isn't optimal while you dink with your gear. It's not that there isn't any restoration occurring when you multi-task–shaking out at a large jug while trying to figure out your next moves certainly restores you somewhat, but it's not very efficient compared to focusing on restoration at that stance without combining it with planning. While the rag doll and body scan physical effects diminish when paired with other tasks, the mental recharge evaporates further still.

Ensure that multi-tasking in these moments is a conscious choice, not your thoughtless default. There are many times when choosing to mix rest with another task is overall the best option for the situation, but take account of the tendency of overestimating the capacity to multi-task in your calculation. Often, while under stress, the tendency to just stop without clear task engagement leaves you in the mushy middle: not doing much of any skill, but a bit of a few, resulting in all the tasks suffering. It takes effort to not just phase out at these moments, instead decisively choosing a goal, then quickly accomplishing it.

Sometimes, a resting position allows achieving multiple goals when the rest position is good enough without ending up in this mushy middle. At these "half and half" locations, you split the pause between exclusive dedication and multitasking by starting with one or the other, then transitioning to the second. At first, for example, you engage in the rest skill such as a rag doll, but you don't use the entire time with this single task. Instead, after, say, half of the time you think you can stay at this stance fully dedicated to restoration, you then switch to multi-tasking: for example, you take three *whoo* exhales of exclusive rag doll when you hit the decent stem rest, concentrating exclusively on deep recovery, but then you take three more *whoo*'s looking upwards, planning your next moves.

In this case, you start yourself off exclusively resting, then multi-task the rest with planning. Front-loading this pause with the rest skill helps carry it forward while you look up-route, deciding what's next. Or, you could reverse the order, which is common when climbing to a clipping stance: your first action is to multi-task the rag doll with clipping, but then you shift your attention 100% to relaxation for the remainder of the time spent at that pause. The key here is to actually remember to delve deeply into the rest instead of half-resting unconsciously.

Practice exclusive attention to restoration skills so that you become a good judge of what full inter-route recovery feels like. Armed with the knowledge of skillfully harnessing your parasympathetic system, you better appraise mixing restoration skills with others, and when you are best served by focusing on restoration alone. Experiment with when to use exclusivity versus multi-tasking to the best advantage.

Unalloyed attention to restoration grants superior psychological resetting, even when there is no physical stress present, such as at large ledges. It seems at these relatively stress free pauses where you can take as long as you want, that your mind would simply clarify on its own, but, while you certainly lower your stress level gratis, it's not as effective as if you work at it. As an example, I once ascended a route that paused at a small precipice below the crux headwall with enough space for me to uncomfortably sit down. After remaining there for several minutes I felt completely physically restored, at which time it occurred to me to actively engage in a three-breath rag doll. After the three *whoo* breaths, I opened my eyes again, surprised at how much more mental clarity and sense of calm returned. Then I took another three-breath closed-eye rag doll, and once again I found myself even more mentally restored, suggesting how active resting techniques benefit the psyche above all.

## Transition quickly and deeply

A critical part of improving at resting is to overcome the natural tendency to want to simply lose focus for a moment when the climbing eases. It makes sense for the psyche that struggled for several difficult moves coupled with a strong dose of fear to want to simply blank out for a moment when the difficulties ease, but this space-out isn't as efficient with this pause than if you engage actively in the rest techniques described here. You want the pause to provide mental and physical repose, but you don't want to just passively relax. Instead, dive deeply and quickly into a rest skill. Instead of just letting the rest "happen," spend attention to getting the most out of it.

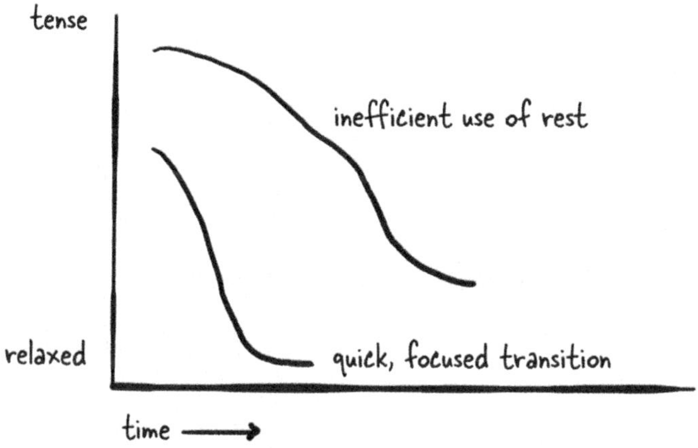


Foster exclusive focus to resting by attending to the initial descent into relaxation. Taking firm, direct action to migrate your mind and body from the tense, locked-in sympathetic systems control while ascending to that of the restorative parasympathetic is a key to wringing the most out of a rest stance. When you hit a rest spot, dramatically declare your intent to yourself to focus 100% on restoration through quickly transitioning, sort of like popping a balloon: as soon as you secure the position, then bang! Release the tension. When we deploy a resting skill while climbing, we often only have a few precious second, sometimes even less. We want to take advantage of these fractions of time by quickly transitioning to the most restful state possible.

The diagram above shows two ways of engaging rest positions. The top line depicts the typical climber who doesn't quickly transition to a rest skill. Without the conscious alternation of focus to the rag doll, we tend to transition slowly to relaxation while not getting very deep into that rest. The bottom line illustrates the ideal rest progression where the climber directly turns his or her attention from the external world to the internal, letting go of any unused muscular tension immediately. It takes full attention to relax your muscles quickly and deeply at rests. By rapidly alternating from climbing to resting when we hit a rest stance, we maximize the restoration afforded by the position. This conscious break-point and precipitous descent encourages exclusivity to the resting skill, so we don't unconsciously start mixing it with, say, wondering what the next move will be.

Quick rests benefit the most from the snappy transition: the faster you release tension, the longer the actual rest. This snappy switch often adds a dramatic increase to the time and intensity of the restoration when the time frame is small. Without the dedicated, purposeful modulation to relaxation, the rest might actually only be two seconds, with it, perhaps double the time.

## *When possible, maximize the rest time*

Physical recovery diminishes over time, requiring increasingly longer durations to gain back the last few percentages of gusto. If you recover 95% in two minutes, this improves to only about 97% in double the time. It might take close to twenty minutes to reach full recovery. The image below illustrates the logarithmic nature of rejuvenation: smaller increments of recovery take increasingly longer time. We get a lot back in short time frames, but the last bits take more than we think. If you really clamp your vasculature down during prolonged, hard efforts, fully recovering might take longer than an hour.

The last bits of recovery take a long time to achieve

Sometimes, you engage in prolonged stressful sequences of climbing where you exert yourself to near exhaustion, at which time you discover a stance that supports a long rag doll. There's a tendency in these moments to under-use this opportunity to calm down. It takes many breaths to fall from the haggard huffing and puffing of exhaustion back down to the easy and calm breathing signifying recovery. Many climbers short-change these rests, starting to climb again far too early. If the stance supports it, monitor your breath, along with your internal sense of the time you can effectively stay at that pause. Listen for the moment where it finally returns to the restful state, then wait several breaths longer before continuing,

Over time, you gain the wisdom of the proper duration: staying at these rests as long as possible, leaving it just before the stance turns to a net-negative. As aptitude at resting improves, you naturally lengthen your stays at these pauses, but you don't stay too long. When you practice this skill, take one more *whoo* breath then you think you need before continuing. When you come down, reflect on how the rest helped or hindered the remaining route. It's likely that during the rest the two or so more breaths seemed too much, but you could actually manages a couple more to positive effect. Continue to explore the correct durations, probing the maximum length that helps you.

At truly sit-down-and-take-a-nap locations, stay far longer than seems intuitive so that you grant your body close to full recuperation. If you find yourself at a truly unlimited rest position such as a big ledge, then use that opportunity to *maximally* recover. With no penalty associated to loitering in that position, take way more time than you think you need. If you feel ready to go in two minutes, then stay four—or even eight. It's likely that you overestimate the pause length in your head (you think five minutes, but it's actually two), so either count the time off to yourself second by second, or, if possible and safe, enlist someone on the ground to start a timer. At truly lie-down-and-snooze locations, camp out so that you grant your body close to full recuperation. When you feel "done," then take a few minutes more.

> Use recovery locations maximally. At unlimited rests, stay far longer than seems natural.

During ascents that really matter, if you climbed non-trivially to a forever-rest, consider taking *really* long breaks in excess of ten minutes or even twenty, granting your body maximal recovery and thus yourself full opportunity to obtain your goal. While a twenty minute duration might only gain you the smallest fraction of additional energy compared to a, say, five minute break, on goal routes, the tiny extra reserve matters, and it takes this significant slice of time to obtain it.

Many climbers encounter difficulty with resting for longer durations due to anxiety. As their mind suddenly finds itself "un-busy" with climbing activities at these big rests, the brain fills with "what if's" and other unhelpful ruminations. They opt to start climbing on partially recovered muscles so that they don't spin out mentally. In instances like this, turn your mind to the meta-skills and resting techniques covered here, particularly with more focused and engrossing proficiencies such as the body scan that requires a lot of mental bandwidth. Keeping your mind occupied with skills sucks all of the air out of the space that might otherwise fuel anxiety, allowing your body full recovery.

# Chapter Four Summary

**Take full advantage of locations to restore your mental and physical energies by quickly and deeply engaging rest skills with your full attention.**

- The rag doll skill combines the *whoo* breath with the *off* gaze for maximal restoration.
- The body scan technique targets hot spots.
- You can use these techniques both at large pause stances and at small ones.
- Practice, as with all skills, results in higher proficiency with these restoration techniques.
- Don't mask indecision and timidity with "rest."
- Focus exclusively on restoration to get the most out of it.
- Transition to recovery as quickly as possible.

Do the following standing on the ground. Then try it just bouldering, like one step off the ground, at a position where you can do a straightforward, full arm extended rest. Close your eyes. Keep them closed.

1. Exhale through your belly and mouth with a relaxing breath. The exhale should be longer than the inhale.

2. Feel the drip of relaxation while you exhale.

3. Visualize the stress draining out of your neck and shoulders as you let your head come down.

4. On the next breath, inhale deeper, then relax deeper on exhale. Feel how much stronger the relaxation of the second breath.

5. Visualize the wax melt of your body as you lower even more into the rest position.

6. Let your head rock back, and your shoulders and back sag, like you are sleeping.

7. Concentrate on letting any tension not required to stay on the wall go. Scan through your body to see if you can feel any tension. Use your attention to relax that spot.

8. Inhale a third time, exhale, and let it all out slowly. Scan through your body again, checking for hot spots.

9. Each exhale typically results in more profound relaxation than the last. You might try experimenting with doing more breaths to see if more or less get you to that ultimate relaxation.

10. Open your eyes slowly.

After some practice on the ground, try it on top-rope or on lead when you feel comfortable closing your eyes. After you come down, tell your partner what the experience was like. Was it relaxing? Did it impact your mental state? Was your attention stable on the rest?

Here are some additional ways to practice resting:

- Experiment on top-rope with how much you can relax. What muscles can you let go of even more than you think.

- On lead in a safe position, rag doll the top jug before clipping.

- On more marginal rests (lead/TR) play around with duration. Try a breath longer or shorter than feels natural and see if you learn something.

- Find a pause and do a small rag doll that slingshots you into the next sequence. The rag doll might only last half a breath, but that half breath 'melt' with the eyes closed is one of the more useful techniques you can have in your arsenal because they are more common than the full rag doll position. Finding these pauses and learning how to get the quick, deep rest can pay off a lot.

- Practice the body scan (refer back to the body scan section earlier in the chapter) on easy routes to get a sense of what it feels like to take stock of the state of your body, then progress to using it at good stances on harder routes.

- On short rests such as those associated with clipping stances, quickly scan through just one area of the body you know you typically carry tension. Focus for that brief moment on releasing muscular tension in only that area. With a *whoo* restorative exhale, feel that tension leave you like air escaping a bag.

- This is a good exercise top-roped so you know there are no fall consequences and can entirely give yourself to this ultimate relaxation practice:

  On an easy route at a good rest stance where you can fully plunge into the rag doll hang, allow more tension release from your body on each subsequent exhale. Take note of the exhale count at which you think you are maximally relaxed, then keep exhaling and relaxing. Allow your hands to relax and open, your weight to keep moving downwards to your feet. Feel the relaxation deepen and your body melt downwards until you naturally fall off the climb. Take note of how much you were pulling with your arms and how more relaxed you were able to get, as well as the number of exhales past your perceived maximum.

# Chapter 5 - Lower Body

The meta-skills (using our eyes and breath), are two actionable ways to marshal intention. In the previous chapter, we built atop those two meta-skills with restoration techniques to recharge the body and mind. Next, we apply meta-skills to the lower body. Our core strength originating from the big muscle groups of the trunk serves as the foundation of strength. The lower body, not the upper, is the base of our climbing power. This chapter explores skills to shift our weight down to the most powerful muscles in our body: the legs, and glutes.

Your awareness is biased to your hands: your lower body seems comparatively far away and removed. The stimulus from your big toe is not as direct as from the index finger. You are much more proficient with your upper body as compared to your lower—your hands more or less run on auto-pilot. Try closing your eyes while climbing on top-rope sometime. You can quickly feel around and effectively use handholds. Not so much for feet. Even when you find a hold to step on, you likely land on a poor part of it. You then end up yarding up the route using your arms a lot more than you would if you could see where to place your foot. When your subconscious doesn't know the *exact* placement your foot, it treats it suspiciously, not pushing to maximal effect.

It's common to see climbers of all ability levels losing track of their lower bodies: scratching at footholds, pogo-sticking unconsciously, barely pushing. But it is the lower body and the comparatively substantial big muscles of your legs and glutes you need to activate as a buttress against the inevitable drain on your forearms as you ascend. In this chapter, the focus turns to improving your mental attention such that you optimally engage the lower body.

The stresses of climbing make the upper body seem like the only thing that matters. By default, we let the lower body run with little attention, concentrating on our hands. Yet our lower body is very incapable of operating with precision when on autopilot, as these muscles lack the fine control of our upper limbs. It takes a lot more concentration to steer these big but dumb muscle groups precisely and use them optimally.

Moreover, the burn and pump of the upper body scream for you to focus even more on *pulling*, even when it's *pushing* with the trunk that is often the better solution. Attending to the lower body sets you up to harness it maximally, reducing the load on your puny forearms. For it to assist you the most effectively, you have to spend a lot of attention on it. Failure to do so ends with you pulling harder than necessary.

## "Technique" almost equals "efficient with lower body"

In this chapter, we focus on the overlap between the mental and technical as it applies to the optimal engagement of the lower body. We often need our best technical abilities right when we tend to chuck them out the window: when stressed. We need to practice technical skills, and we need to practice harnessing them under duress. This helps drive these skills down deep into our subconscious, availing them to us at times when we require their assistance the most.

To a large degree, what we mean by the term *technical* is the efficient deployment of the lower body. The term *technique* denotes biomechanical efficiency, ways of moving the body that use less muscle per ascending centimeter. While this could refer to *any* way of finding biomechanical advantage, such as the use of a hand jam, it typically refers to finding ways to pass weight down to the mighty trunk. We want to employ the lower body as quickly and thoroughly as possible as to save the comparatively wimpy upper body.

PRACTICE

On top-rope, find a smallish foothold to practice. First try blindly finding that foot and pushing on it. Next time keep your eyes on it until it's fully weighted. Notice how much more you feel you can push on the hold when you kept your eyes on it.

Climbing deceives us. It seems like the upper body is pulling us up the climb, but it's really the lower body (the large muscles of the legs and glutes) that are *pushing* the load. The most significant reason for this confusion is that the effort we put forth from our fingers is much closer to their maximum. Our lower body, by comparison, is typically working well within its capacity. The result is that our forearms are loud while our lower bodies stoically and quietly carry out their task. The natural tendency is to attend to the noisiest muscles.

De-couple the stimulus of the forearms from your response to that stimulus. Train yourself to look for ways of relieving the forearms by better use of your lower body.

The graph on the next page illustrates the differences between the two worlds—the lower and upper halves of our body. Pretend a climber is ascending an ordinary sequence of moves. This average sequence will be well within the capacity of her lower body, but close to maximum load on the forearms. The feedback from her prime movers is minimal, while that from the fingers rises from uncomfortable to significant.

Even when considering routes where our lower body tires, such as a long box corner that flames your calves, the sense of unease raised from torched legs or feet pales in comparison to the abject panic of a pumped forearm. The comparatively large leg muscles, even when taxed, spreads the load among many more individual muscle fibers—we can carry on considerably longer through pumped legs than pumped arms. It's exceedingly rare for a climber to fall off a route due to trunk muscle failures.

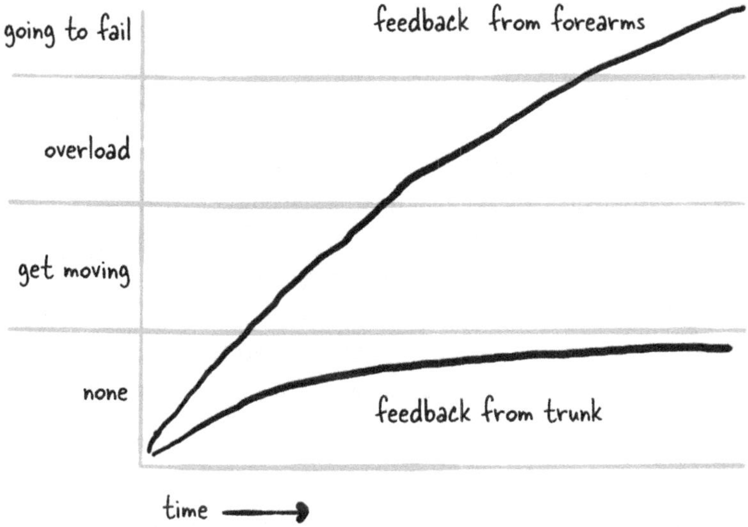


Above a certain level, the feedback from muscles starts to raise alarms to our consciousness. Below this threshold, we have little to no awareness whatsoever that they are doing anything, as the graph above suggests. The closer that muscle gets to maximum load, the more it will signal that there's a potential problem. This may rise to the point where the feedback becomes overwhelming, drowning out all else—as in the classic fully flamed forearm pump. The problem is that we over-correlate this signal—the problem—with our *response*.

We strongly associate the feeling of urgency from our burning forearms with *taking even more action with our forearms*! In the moments where we feel the seemingly impossible to ignore signals from our fingers, it's challenging to focus our attention elsewhere. Most often, the scream from our forearms should prompt us to take action by engaging the large trunk muscles to take more of the load—not even more from the forearms. When we feel the burn, we should want to immediately concentrate more on our trunk and *pushing.*

Where it seems that climbing is all about finger and forearm strength, it's more accurate to say it is about linking the power of the lower body to the upper. Generally, we climb by positioning ourselves in place with our hands so that we can wind up and push again with our core. Our arms are *assistive*: their job is more to keep us in place until the lower body can push us upwards again. This is perhaps the most significant misdirection in our sport: climbing is usually about *pushing with our legs*, not *pulling with our arms.*

There are certainly moves and routes where we support the majority of our weight by our upper body, but most of the time, it is our trunk that is supporting the majority of our weight. The exception proves the rule. For routes that use a lot of forearm, *it is even more critical* to use our lower body as much as possible to keep the forearm pump at bay. The small margin common on these sorts of routes means that the measly forearms need all the help they can get, and that help primarily comes from the trunk. Counter-intuitively, the steeper the climbing, the more lower body engagement helps. Any forearm relief we may provide improves our chances for success.

PRACTICE

Climb an easy route concentrating on this wave of power that originates with your lower body, transfers through your core, and materializes as you propel yourself towards the hold. Feel the linkage of energy springing you upwards.

# Attentive Foot Placement

The most important way of generating more force and getting more engagement from our workhorse muscles in the lower body is through the mindful application of the foot. For it is the first link in the power train. If this connection to the rock is suspect, we will not use it to full advantage. Moreover, as we will see in a moment, how we choose to place our feet on the rock dictates the direction we can send that power and reach upwards. Our hands can run on autopilot: it typically does not take a lot of concentration to identify and accurately use a handhold. Our feet are a totally different story.

Under times of stress, you need to turn exclusive focus to your feet. They act as the sentinel of the lower body. The foot is key to unlocking the power in your trunk. Turn the focus to the feet through your eyes, for, as you learned with clipping in **Chapter 2**, narrowing your gaze down to about a thumbnail square or smaller with the pinpoint gaze provides an actionable target for your foot. Like clipping, you don't want to look blandly at the foothold, but, instead, really zero in on the *exact* target.

PRACTICE

On a route with less than stellar feet, practice keeping your eyes on each foot until you weight it. Only then allow yourself to change your gaze.

You can generally direct your hands to a target and then almost forget about them. They will nearly always act optimally even with a rather low level of attention. Not so with our feet. They require much more direction to aim, fire the muscles to land them on the target, load them with precision so that they don't blow off the hold, then push optimally. Treat your feet like small children: they need constant monitoring and specific direction. They tend to wander off task. Focus *attention* on the feet, allow your *awareness* to manage your hands.

If you take the extra half-second to follow through your foot placement with your eyes so you begin weighting it before changing the direction of your gaze, you confirm to your subconscious that the foot can be used to full effect. Granting your dumb big muscles concrete specificity by telling them *exactly* where to go ensures they in turn power you upwards maximally. In short, you want to apply the same techniques we learned with the pinpointing a clip in **Chapter 2** to our feet. Start with *pinpoint* focus of the eyes (see the **drill** at the end of this chapter). Continue through remaining narrowly focused on that target while you firmly and accurately place your foot *exactly* where you intend. It's easy to shortchange this attention.

## *Don't lose track of your lower body*

Many climbers, perhaps most, look at the foothold but then direct their attention elsewhere just before their foot makes contact with the rock. Keeping your eyes focused on the foot until you confirm it secure is a primary way of gaining efficiency with your lower body. Any additional push from your trunk is a decrease in equal proportion in pulling with your forearms.

Climbers generally overestimate how much attention they are paying to their feet. They look at their foot, watching it get very close to placement on the hold, but a split second before their foot actually makes contact, they turn their eyes to the next limb. Others put their foot on, then bounce or slide around as if they were pogo-sticking on the hold when their attention is elsewhere. No good can come of moving your foot without your eyes on it.[1] Identify and work to eliminate looking away from your foot until you begin shifting your weight to it and positively engage it physically. You want your lower limbs to act like rigid poles. Bouncing or shifting around on a foothold is a recipe for blowing off, and suggests that you aren't using your lower body maximally. As soon as your eyes leave your foot, it should remain a rigid structure, like a pier of a bridge. Our foot, much like how a column supports a structure, is the foundation for the remainder of our body.

> Don't move your foot unless you are looking at it.

The mind registers any uncertainty of complete and secure foot contact by resisting pushing as hard as it would if it felt 100% about the placement. Part of our subconscious worries about it failing. We want to get every last ounce of weight off our forearms—5% better engagement of your lower body is nearly identical in effect to a 5% strength increase in your fingers. Focusing on your foot placement is the principal means of building this bridge of

---

[1] *Except, of course, when the terrain is such that you can't see your foot, or when you consciously rotate on a hold.*

power. Using your attention, lock down the connection to the stone at your toes. Convince your subconscious that it is trustworthy before shifting your attention to the next mechanic. With that certainty baked in, your legs can take all the load available to them.

Some climbers lose track of their lower body as they ascend. They start somewhat attentive to foot engagement, yet as they then turn their eyes upwards, their lower body takes on a life of its own. This inattention manifests in actions such as unconscious calf bobbing or even taking the foot entirely off the hold to just scratch blindly at the wall. Others think they are being conscious of the foot placement, but are so impatient to get past the attention to their feet and on to the "real climbing" with their arms that they end up tapping their toes around on the hold, not entirely mentally engaged

# Keeping Attention on Target

Natasha pinpoints her gaze at the foot target, keeping it unwaveringly locked on the bullseye as she starts to move her foot to meet it.

Her eyes remain locked on target while she begins placing her foot. In the split second as she starts transferring weight to it, she takes quick note of feeling, the firm connection taking shape.

Only after registering positive contact on the foothold does she then allow her eyes to move to the next hold.

as they weight their foot. They are looking at the foot placement, but are so anxious to get on with their burning forearms that they cut the mental attention short. The net result is that the weight that could transmit to the trunk winds up burdening the already overtaxed forearms. Many climbers who suffer from this problem are unaware of it. If you suspect you might be losing track of your lower body, ask a partner you trust to observe you on a non-trivial route, or video yourself.

Partial attention to foot placements such as this "patty-cakes" tap dance or foot drift suggests underlying anxiety. Perhaps the climber is overly goal-oriented or fear motivated—he's concerned if he "wastes time" looking at his foot he will fall off with burning forearms in a few more moves. While it's certainly understandable that these emotions and subconscious thoughts arise, it's ultimately counterproductive to continue to grant short shrift to foot placements. If you suffer from this hitch, then it is doubly important to practice keeping your intentions on your lower body. In lower stress situations, fortify the habit of engaging your lower body completely. You improve your state of mind by acting on these small physical manifestations. When you lock down your limbs so they are reliable foundations, you decrement anxiety as a side-effect.

As Natasha eyes the target hold, her right foot begins to bob up and down, reflecting her inner anxiety of the move. She can help calm her anxiety by noticing this unwanted movement, locking it down.

If you find yourself falling victim to this sort of anxiety, here's an antidote: on easier routes, just stressful enough to provoke this overly-attentive-to-the-upper-body reaction, practice shunting enough attention down through your lower body to take stock of how it's doing. Much like the body scan drill from the previous chapter, taking a quick moment to check in with your lower body at regular intervals helps build a mentality that is not overly attentive to just the arms. We need our entire body engaged effectively. The lower body needs regular, refreshed attention to serve you well in ascent.

Of course, not all footholds require the same level of attention—some compel less than full focus: that big jug doesn't likely need much care for you to push efficiently on it. This is one way that a steady diet of climbing plastic can often be detrimental to learning lower body engagement at the foot, as epoxy holds often have very forgiving foot placements. If you climb a lot on artificial holds, put increased emphasis on finding routes with poor footholds, or make existing routes harder by choosing worse aspects of the holds to force yourself to use, say, a lousy side crystal instead of the big blob at the top of the hold.

## *Stay lower-body engaged: some tips*

- A technique that can help counteract the innate clumsy nature of our lower body is to **exaggerate the movement**. This exaggeration is another way of focusing attention. Instead of merely moving the foot to the next hold, consciously apply some "art" to it, as if you were a ballerina. Say for example you have a foot target far off to the left. As you lift your left foot to place it, extend it out in the air and point your big toe in space at the hold in the orientation you want it when it lands, then surgically touch it down on the target. Using a flourish like this can serve to intensify the attention to your foot.

- **Get interested in the small details** of the foot placement. Help hone the strong but dumb legs into precision instruments. Applying interest and attention to your foot placements is the most significant way you can further empower your lower body. Climbing is a skill-based sport. It requires a lot of attention and awareness, nowhere more so than in reacting to the feeling of forearm burn. Practice responding to the stimulus of pump by tuning into your lower body through precision foot placements. Counter-intuitively, when the sense of burn starts escalating, you need to respond by *slowing down slightly*, carefully identifying footholds, applying concentration to stepping on them properly, and following through with your eyes remaining on the hold while you weight it. It takes a lot of practice to inculcate this response to forearm pump or general exhaustion.

- Put a **centimeter wide strip of tape at the end of your shoe** (cleaning the rubber with a little alcohol swab helps it stick) pointing forward like your big toe. While climbing, look at footholds where you will be placing the front of your foot, then match that tape strip like a gun sight on the centimeter of the foothold you target. The bit of tape helps hone your eye to the exact focus. Additionally, a white tape strip stands out as a clear sight picture that grabs your eye as you look downwards. It's a not-so-subtle reminder to attend to precision.

- **Engage in the *wha* breath** while turning your attention to the foot placement. Use the stress-dispersing benefit of this skill to help decrease anxiety.

- **Ask a trusted climbing partner to critique your attentiveness** to your feet. With all the stimulus of climbing, it's easy to think you are doing a better job than you are. Get a reality check from someone you trust. Have them give you an honest and accurate evaluation of how they see you attending to your feet.

- **Reflect on how well you did** after the route. Immediately upon hitting the ground, run through the route in your mind, replaying your attentiveness to your feet. Are there blank spots where you can't remember your foot placements?

# The Mystery of Load Balance

Deliberate, focused, pinpoint precision of the feet eases anxiety, allowing you to fully engage your lower body, positioning yourself with optimal biomechanical advantage. We push harder when we pinpoint the foot, but most of us don't have a good understanding of what it means to engage fully with the trunk. Typically, we just put the foot down, and we sort of magically end up standing on it. There's an internal regulation system that balances out pushing with the lower body and pulling with the hands. This regulation system is entirely subconscious. How is it that our subconscious decides to divvy up the load? This is an interesting field to explore:

- The lower body is a fire-and-forget system. We must practice *aiming* this system properly, but after we pull the trigger, we can turn our attention elsewhere. The lower body is generally solid from then on.

- The upper body requires less effort to manage—it seems almost an extension of our will. It's quicker and more nuanced. We can command it easily and subtly, but we must cycle our attention back regularly to refresh our intent, due to the alarming feeling of pump.

Those who work individual routes or boulder problems many times experience how much easier the movements become with repeated attempts. While it's difficult to measure, a lot of the sense of decreasing difficulty that we feel as we learn this efficiency on a given sequence of moves is our neurophysiological system adapting to allowing the lower body to take up more of the load. For it stands to reason that if we aren't pulling as hard with our hands, then our weight must be supported elsewhere—for virtually every move, the only other place that could carry the load is our trunk.

Oddly, it doesn't *feel* as if our lower body takes up the slack; our subconscious allows our overtaxed forearms to relax, transferring this weight to our feet, but the sensation is just that it feels less difficult to pull with our hands. We notice the *decrease* in work in our arms, but we don't notice the *increase* of effort from our lower body. Take note of this phenomenon the next time you climb a route multiple times—how your subconsciousness automatically learn to shift some of the load from your hands to your feet. Are there ways you could *consciously* shift even more of the weight off your arms? Perhaps, with practice, we can move the set point such that it directs more weight to our trunk straight away instead of overkilling it with the forearms.

# Feet Direct Your Orientation

When people talk about climbing 'technique,' they are typically referring to a mechanic that starts with how you place your foot on the hold. This placement sets the stage for musculoskeletal system. The vast majority of foot placements in climbing engage the front part of the foot. Of those front of the foot placements, most occur on the inside or big-toe edge. A smaller amount of placements are directly on the front nose point, then likely smaller still on the outside pinky toe side (as in a back-step).

The rotation of your foot dictates your orientation to the rock. If you fan your arms out on the wall in a right back-step, you have several inches of wall you can touch on the right that you can't reach if you rotate to a left back-step. Not only is the reach shifted from side to side, but the biomechanics are different. Your skeleton is also oriented dramatically differently, resulting in movement advantages and disadvantages depending on the situation. The common 'both inside edge' position for your feet may be the best solution for a given problem, or it might not be. It has strengths and weaknesses, just like left and right back-steps. The steeper the stone in general, the more back-steps tend to help you get your hips closer to the wall. It also helps you extend in a 'twist-lock' position as you rotate your body towards one side.

Thus, placing yourself in the optimal position for a given move starts with your foot's orientation to the wall. If the scenario dictates 'both inside edge,' then you want to place yourself intentionally that way. But perhaps a right or left back-step, or maybe a front-point, is ideal. You need to identify your best guess and intentionally set your foot so that as you weight it, it directs your hips and thus your upper body into that mechanically superior position for the given sequence.

## *Don't always mimic a starfish*

The 'both inside edge' movement pattern of climbing has the advantage of being very close to the way humans walk on the ground. It puts a lot of the force a little farther back on the big toe, which is strong, sensitive, more flexible, and more under your conscious control than the rest of your foot. It keeps you in a neutral position compared to back-stepping, not shifted to the left or right. Unfortunately, since your feet are both rotated somewhere around 45 degrees (or even less) outwards, that means that your butt must go out away from the wall in direct response to your knees rotating into the wall. This results in your weight not centered directly over your feet, causing more stress on the forearms. This *starfish* movement pattern may be the best position for a given movement, but it isn't the best for *all* actions. However, it dominates the orientation most climbers take to the stone. For some climbers, there is no other orientation. Why is that?

If you draw a line down your body from head to toe, splitting yourself in two, then another across your body below your arms, you create a quadrant. The upper left is your left shoulder/arm/hand, the lower-left the remainder of your body, mirrored by the right side. This is a pretty apt depiction of our awareness as we have discussed at length so far: our arms get a massive percentage of the focus, and the rest almost nothing. The lower quadrants are distant and remote.

We tend to move according to habit, our limbs staying in their regular quadrant. Practicing non-starfish movements helps us continue to pick the optimal body position even when stressed.

We can teach ourselves foreign movements, but under times of stress, we will tend to revert to the most familiar patterns, well worn from years or decades of use. Non-starfish patterns are somewhat stressful. Even those well-versed in crossing the midline with their feet tend to stop doing so when on-sight climbing. The percentage of back-steps decrease with stress. The more you train non-starfish movement patterns, the more available they become in these moments. Since various other body orientations (hookings, back-steps, and flags for example) can be vastly superior to front-on starfishing for a given situation, the more foot placement-related movement patterns you practice under increasing stress, the better. It's not that moving like a starfish is terrible per se, it just may not be *optimal* for a given sequence. You want to mindfully *choose* the starfish pattern out of many because it is the *best* solution to the given problem, regardless of the stress or anxiety level.

Of course, an inexpertly applied cross-movement or any other non-starfish pattern is likely a worse choice than going frog-legged. A lot of newer climbers will mimic what they see other better climbers doing, such as drop knees. It's likely how we all learned some of the non-intuitive movements in climbing. However, while they get their limbs pointed in the correct direction, their lack of strength and confidence results in a back-step that is less effective than if they had starfished it.

> It takes conscious intention to continue to choose optimal movement patterns under duress.

# Chapter Five Summary

**Our lower body is our power center, but it often gets usurped by the cranky forearms. Practice lower body engagement starting with attention at your feet to take as much burden off your arms as possible.**

- We aren't very aware of our lower body. Compensate by consciously granting attention to it.
- The mind by default responds to the sirens from the forearms, but often we should countermand this instinct by attending to the lower body.
- Use the pinpoint gaze on specific targets to place feet. Follow through.
- Lower body "wanderings" reflect inner anxiety. Counteract this by doubling your efforts to mold your lower body into a rigid support structure.
- The way you place your feet dictates the way you orient to the wall. Practice different movement patterns starting with varying orientations of the foot so they are available under stress.

The following drill practices using your eyes to sharpen the mental focus onto your body in orientation to the wall. This is a fundamental drill that climbers of all abilities can return to fruitfully. Like we discussed in the clipping drills, the *regular* gaze is usually not optimal. We need to change it consciously to the *pinpoint*.

On an easy route, either top-roped or on lead, run through the following **for each foot placement**. Note that the first few times through this drill, you are likely to skip steps by accident. Do a route, then come down and re-read the drill steps. The steps you can't remember are likely keys to weaknesses in your climbing, so pay particular attention to what you are consistently missing—you might stumble onto something that you can improve quickly! A lot is going on in this drill. It will take a few routes to settle into it, so give yourself space to get focused on the mechanics mentality by picking an easy enough route so you can concentrate on the steps.

1. Bring 100% focus with your eyes to the target foothold. Be specific, targeting a centimeter or so circle.

2. Notice yourself start to put your foot exactly where you want it. Do it with intention and concentration using the pinpoint gaze.

3. Exaggerate the foot placement as if you were performing surgery. Place it as if you're landing a helicopter filled with nitroglycerin gently on the pad.

4. Step up slowly, feeling the transition onto that hold. Take note of your foot engagement. It's way down there, remote and somewhat vague. Keep your attention to that feeling.

5. Take note of the feeling of engaging your lower body. Think of that link on the stone starting at the tip of your toe/foot then transitioning through your legs, core, then upper body, arms, then, finally, onto the hand holds. Feel that bridge from lower to the upper body.

6. Keep your eyes on that foothold as you transition your weight onto it. Keep your awareness on your lower body. **Follow through** on the foothold with your eyes.

7. Do not take your eyes off until you are ON the foothold. You need your eyes on target until the foot is really, truly engaged. Take note of what that foot pressure feels like when you register that you are on that hold. Only then take your eyes off, directing them to the next limb. In that split second where you transition your weight to that foot, take note of where you feel you are "on" it, then you can switch your concentration elsewhere.

8. Keep some concentration on that foot as you continue to move. Do not allow your foot to change—no ankle bobs or scooting. Your foot and leg are rigid as a pillar, pushing and delivering that lower body power upwards.

Here are some more things to work on as you get through the basic lower body attention drill:

- Do the previous foot placement drill, but keep count of any foot placements that aren't inside edge. Are you always a starfish? If you are nearly always starfishing, try routes while looking for and accomplishing back-steps or other non-starfish patterns. What kind of novel ways of using your feet can you come up with?

- On easy routes during your warm-up in the gym do the foot placement drill, choosing worse feet than you would normally use. You can pick chips or just use part of a big hold instead of stomping on the biggest part. Try to find novel ways of placing your feet: front edge, toe straight on, back edge.

- On top-rope on an *easy* route, perform continuous up/down-climbing for between 15-30 minutes. As you tire, you will notice that it's harder to focus on your feet. Force yourself to focus your consciousness down on your feet using the pinpoint gaze, continuing to place your feet surgically. Have your belay partner be on the lookout for when you start to lose foot focus, gently calling you back to the drill. Stay concentrated on your foot placements, using that surgical precision and concentration on prime mover engagement, even if you fall off.

- On medium-hard routes (ones where you can divert enough attention to thinking outside the physical act of climbing itself), keep tally of any times you lost track of your lower body. Some climbers nearly campus themselves up routes, particularly if they get really stressed. Take note of any time where you find yourself bobbing a foot, chicken scratching, or moving your foot unconsciously.

- On a medium/easy route on top-rope or lead, focus on feeling your core as you ascend. It's hard to listen to your abs and back with all the other stimuli. Cultivate being able to hear what your core is doing. Are you fully engaging it? Do the route again, but exaggerate your core strength by hip thrusting, pushing your lower back towards the wall, and tightening your abs. This will likely feel really foreign.

- Easy route (TR/lead): pay attention to how much you are really pushing. Try raising your heel just a bit to see if that helps you engage your lower body more. This is a subtle thing that may take a little bit of experimenting with to get that "in your bones" intuition. It's hard to get your lower body to push harder as it always seems to be on autopilot.

- Medium difficulty route on top-rope: on the most marginal foot holds, see how much you can push before you pop off. Experiment with not putting as much of your shoe on the hold to see how much more marginal that could be and still be useful.

- Find opportunities on easy and medium routes to explore ways of crossing the midline with your hands and feet. This may be exploring different ways of back-flagging (like at a clip), or 'stepping through': your right foot actually steps to the left of the left foot (or the left steps to the right of the right foot). Again, while the flag or step-through may not be the most optimal way of moving for that route, the goal is to practice the novel movements, not be the most efficient on this particular route.

- As you climb, it's probable that you will get distracted from lower body awareness. As soon as you notice that you are not focused on the lower body, gently return your awareness to it. The stimulus from our forearms drowns out awareness of the lower body. It can take some time to learn how to listen to what your body is saying below your armpits.

- Our trunk is much stronger than our forearms. Even if we aren't pushing very hard with it, every ounce we can remove from our comparatively weak forearms helps. The first step in engaging our lower body is becoming more aware of how we orient it. On an easy climb (less than .10-), simply pay attention to how your lower body feels. Direct your attention to picking up the feelings of insecurity, power, balance, or whatever else originates from your base.

# Chapter 6 - Assembly

So far, we've discussed a set of skills in a hierarchy, a pyramid with the foundation of meta-skills followed by a layer consisting of lower body engagement and recovery techniques, all built atop the substrate of mindfulness. In this chapter, we complete the triangle with *assembly* procedures. These are ways we formulate movement plans, stitching them together into an unbroken whole. Where each skill is like a *link*, we want to assemble these links into a continuous *chain*. Through this, we keep our mind engrossed.

Another way of looking at an *assembly* is to consider it a catch-all term that encompasses both *tactics* and *strategy*. A *tactic* is a small, rudimentary set of steps to accomplish a well-defined goal, where a *strategy* is an overall approach to reach a larger end. In terms of climbing, an example of a tactic would be to, say, skip the last bolt of a route on a redpoint attempt because you know the fall is safe and you save three critical seconds not clipping it. A climbing strategy is an overall approach to ascending the line, like maximizing every rest position, or climbing as quickly as possible.

This chapter investigates how to assemble plans into tactics, then how to evolve these tactics into an overall strategy. In climbing, we look at this in terms of *beta*, which we turn to next.

## Beta Scripts and Chains

As you approach your maximum physical capability, you enter a realm where the mind proportionally plays a more significant role in determining success or failure. Sometimes just slightly more effort can make a huge difference. Focus dims under stress, right when we need our highest degree of psychic acumen to counteract the desire to stop or to suppress the feedback of a pump. This means that much like we manage muscular pump, we want to cultivate the ability to manage and re-invigorate our psyche. Small, marginal mental improvements can mean a lot, particularly if that small improvement granted by enhanced mental fortitude gets you past the one stopper move. A powerful technique that helps ease the mind and manage mental fatigue during difficult times is *beta scripting.*

## Beta, defined

Before looking closely at beta scripts, let's define terms. *Beta* is a catch-all for details about climbing moves. It could refer to just a single move or even only part of a move, from a key little description of a hold to grab, all the way up to a minute account of every detail of a whole route with dozens of subtleties. This amorphous definition clutters understanding the different ways we formulate and use beta. Let's, therefore, clarify the meaning of *beta* for our purposes here before moving on.

1. A **beta script** is a detailed plan for movement through **just a handful of moves**, or less, about the quantity of a single bolt length. This script could be the result of working out the moves many times when climbing in the redpoint style, or it might be a provisional plan with options when scoping moves you don't know when climbing in the on-sight mode. The script may consist of just climbing moves, or it could include meta-skills such as a breath skill or any of the other techniques discussed in this book. A script is roughly analogous to a *tactic.*

2. A **beta chain**, assembles the short but more featured *scripts* into a **coherent whole from the bottom to the top** of a climb. Since not every move requires the same level of exacting detail as the more difficult or tricky sections, we typically don't need granular specifications for the *entire* route that more formal scripts provide. We *chain* together beta scripts of the climbing moves by filling in the blank spots with the skills covered in this book.

Making the distinction between *scripts* and *chains* maps well to our mental hardware. The mind can only keep a handful of details in working memory. The beta script is about that size. Since a critical way of managing hard tasks is to break them down into smaller parts, think specifically about script-sized goals while ascending. However, if we just left it at the handful of moves a script represents, then the blank spaces *in between* these detailed plans may lose shape or focus. That's where the chain concept, discussed shortly, comes to play. Think of scripts as bite-sized, chains the whole enchilada. Thus, an assembled chain becomes the *strategy* to accomplish the climb.

As a thought experiment, consider a route you attempt on-sight with a series of 6-9 moves (roughly the limit of working memory), followed by a great rest. This arrangement repeats itself for the entirety of the line. This allows you to follow the pattern:

1. Look at the next series of moves to figure out your best guess through them, with perhaps an alternate plan or two should your first guess not match reality.

2. Execute the plan.

3. Engage a recovery skill,

4. Repeat step 1.

This idealized route allows you to formulate a beta script, execute it, then engage in a full rest in a cycle. The route is like a series of boulder problems. You chain together beta scripts by two skills (resting and planning), then repeat. Every moment is taken up by either engaging entirely with actual movement, or a meta-skill. It matches your mental hardware well, allowing you to switch fully to the slow System 2 thinking to prepare a beta script, use it while engaging in the System 1 mode, then physically and mentally recover. In this idealized example, the climb splits into divisions mapping well to how the brain processes information. You plan with the well-rested and slower analytical brain—System 2—then execute the plan in the intuitive mode—System 1. This illustrates how you assemble beta scripts into a full chain for a complete route.

Of course, few routes map this well to the mind. In the real world, you make compromises, but this idealized route shows the basic pattern. Many, if not most, routes break down into a rough approximation of this ideal, particularly when climbing in the redpoint style.

## *Scripts grease the gears*

Let's start the exploration of *beta scripting* with an example. Say Maya has been working a difficult gym route for several days, getting close to the redpoint. She's now encountering problems just before the last bolt, where she must pull three small crimps in a row on the steepest part of the wall. Given the accumulation of mental and physical fatigue to this point, Maya finds it seemingly too difficult to lock onto the second of these crimps. As she grabs it, the biofeedback from her forearm causes her to freeze momentarily from the difficulty. With the distressing feedback from her hand, she can't think about bringing her left foot up to a good block, the next move to follow. This lock-up exemplifies how Maya's physical and mental limits hit the red-line simultaneously. We can't do anything about our *physical* limitations in the short term, but we can take action to counteract issues of the mind.

Before her next attempt, Maya pre-loads her short term memory with a *beta script* as a way to give her mind a quick antidote to apply when she hits that second crimp:

> "It's going to feel so not-doable when I hit that hold, but that's OK. I've done that move several times after resting on the rope. I know how to pull it. The only thing different is the pump now. So when I hit the hold, and it feels horrible, I'm going to then pinpoint my eyes down to the foot block, engaging it no matter how my arms feel."

With this, Maya combats the physical and mental problem at the last bolt with a plan. This plan contains acceptance of how the move will feel as an end-run around the part of her mind that she knows will yell at her to stop. Note that this script contains both mechanical details about the physical moves, but also psychological primers. She's implicitly saying to herself that while a sub-mind is going to tell her that continuing at that moment isn't possible, she is going to accept that voice on advisement and then turn her eyes to her feet.

> Strong plans prepare the mind so it is less reactive to internal and external stimulus.

Concocting a specific plan such as this reduces the mental circuitry processing the inbound stimulus at that critical juncture. Maya knows that the second crimp is going to incur temporary paralysis, so she plans a direct counter-action: strong engagement with the *pinpoint* gaze. With this decisive intent, she bypasses the parts of her brain that would react to and make decisions about that inbound stimulus. There's no space granted to thoughts like "oh that feels too hard." While she can't turn off the biofeedback, she can, through quickly turning her gaze to the next target, shape her mind so that it is less reactive to it.

Meta-skills are great options to choose in reaction to pitfalls of the mind such as this strong upwelling of "I can't go on" because they deploy so quickly. By scheming to react to the jolt of maximal muscular effort when she hits that problematic hold by immediately pinpointing the foot block, Maya allows that distressing message to pass through her while she initiates the next move. The pinpoint gaze meta-skill counters the potentially overwhelming shock of grabbing the first crimper.

This movement script is not guaranteed to succeed, of course. It increases the chances, though, through Maya acknowledging her mental process ("it's going to feel so not-doable") coupled with a concrete action: pinpointing her next foot target. In other words, she sets herself up so that when part of her mind tells her to stop, she will *take one more action* instead.

When you hear the inner voice telling you to stop, make just one more move.

A byproduct of countering strong biofeedback with a meta-skill is the deepening of your suspicion that the messages that seemed so convincing—"there's no way I can pull that crimp"—lose a bit of their power. They appear like only another piece of information, not *the truth*. Hard climbing exposes the liminal space where the mental and physical intersect. The beta script is a sort of mental hack whereby we partially bypass neural networks that otherwise cause us to seize up.

Remember back in **Chapter 1** where we discussed the nature of anxiety through the example of a bored dog who, left alone too long, tears the sofa to shreds. With the beta script, you help decrease the time your mind has to think about the experience, keeping the stir-crazy internal dog at bay. You instead prime your mind to act immediately. On the margin, where success or failure hangs in the balance, you want to keep the fast, intuitive body piloting the ship. This is not a time to slow down and contemplate. While we often hear the maxim "listen to your body," there are times like this where we want to *ignore* it to the fullest extent possible. We only have a few *milliseconds* separating continuation from falling. The beta script incurred the thinking and planning by the slower but more methodical System 2 up front. You then execute the moves when you trigger your beta script off, keeping the slow analytic mind on the back burner.

Recall beta scripts before you start climbing, but also as close as possible to when you need it, preferably *right* before beginning the moves in the plan. "Athletes can 'load' their working memory voluntarily with certain information to control their attentional focus."[1] Short term memory is a bit like a mountain. You put intention on top of it, and it immediately starts sliding downhill away from you. While Maya formulates a concise and easily actionable script on the ground, her mind is going to load up with all sorts of strong stimulus in the moment as she climbs. This overload pushes the script farther downhill in memory, rendering it more difficult to recall. With hard climbing, your mental resources are just about wholly tapped out dealing with all the kinesthetic input. With so much stimulus bombarding you on harder climbs, your mind encounters difficulty quickly loading up the details of the movement scheme. Help the beleaguered brain by preloading short term memory with your script as close as possible to when we will use it. This helps the critical details from sliding far down the hill.

Most routes have at least some sort of pause in the action. This may not be at an ideal location right before you want to recall the beta script. On Maya's route, an uncomfortable sloping side-pull a bolt before the three-crimp crux allows her enough time to look up at the foot block she wants to pinpoint with her eyes up at the crux. Ideally, she'd run through the script much more vividly closer to using it, but this pause stance doesn't allow it, and there isn't one closer. So she chooses the vital part of her beta script at this pause: pinpointing that foot block. This repositions the most critical part of the script back to the summit of her memory, granting the highest chance that the little details she needs come to life while climbing through those crimps.

---

[1]*Furley Philip & Schweizer, Geoffrey & Bertrams, Alex. (2015). The two modes of an athlete. Dual-process theories in the field of sport, p 2. International Review of Sport and Exercise Psychology. 10.1080/1750984X.2015.1022203.*

The tried-and-true memorization technique of developing a mnemonic as a shorthand helps a lot at these sub-optimal pauses. Perhaps Maya, instead of just pinpointing the foot block, might have enough time at the uncomfortable side-pull to remember the little jingle she put together that encapsulates the crux sequence. She says to herself "one, two, three, foot, foot" as a quick and evocative stand-in for the full beta: pull the three crimps, then make the two foot moves. The phrase doesn't need to make sense to anyone else but her as long as it roots the essential details in her brain. This mnemonic is easy to recall and forces the five-move sequence to the top of her memory stack. Moreover, the simple phrase doesn't take the slower System 2 mind to digest, allowing her to stay in the quick intuition of System 1. While it's not quite as powerful as fully visualizing a beta script, it's the best option when the pause doesn't afford a full recounting.

So far, we've described beta scripting when you already know the moves, but you can also script for on-sight climbing. In the previous example, Maya knew the difficulties and thus "wrote" a script with specific countermeasures. She knew what to do. The script reminds her what it feels like and how to handle the brain lock-up when it inevitably hits. When you don't know the route, the script is concocted on the fly, with options when possible.

Say Maya is halfway up a challenging on-sight in an uncomfortable stem rest. The sequence to the next bolt is anxiety-producing: she can't tell if the future series of holds are slopers or if they might be positive around the bulbous sides. That leaves her with trepidation regarding her next clipping stance. Though uncomfortable, Maya has enough time in this stem to look forward through the sloping section to devise a plan. Maya uses this good stance to turn entirely to System 2, carefully scoping the slopers. She formulates a script to handle the possibility that she is going to feel physically and mentally maxed-out through this sloper sequence:

> "I can see the hold two feet above the next draw is good enough to clip. I'd really like to clip it three moves before that, but I'm not sure that hold is positive enough. So what I'll do is hit that lower sloper and immediately decide if it's good enough. I'm not going to spend more than a half second making that decision. If it's not positive, I'm going to the big locker crimp above the bolt and clip from my waist. The fall is safe, and it's really not much longer if I fall from the higher hold."

By taking the time to sketch out a scheme beforehand, complete with safety analysis, Maya prepares her mind so that there isn't much thinking to do when she's climbing the moves. Anticipating that she may find herself spending too much mental and physical energy figuring out the sloper sequence while in the midst of it, she devises a plan that eases the thought process when she's maxed-out. When she hits the slopers, she doesn't have to think. She just makes the snap judgment fully re-engaged in System 1.

In these two examples, Maya's fully fleshed out her inner dialog as if she's narrating it to someone. While this is something of a contrivance as a means to describe this internal process in this book, it's important to note that when you have the wherewithal to do so, talking to yourself in semi-complete sentences helps solidify the plan. *Literally saying the words* makes thoughts run through additional neural pathways. This at once adds extra processing power, so the plan makes more sense to your mind while also strongly embedding the script in memory.

In Maya's on-sight example, stemming uncomfortably below the row of slopers, it's likely more realistic that her script is a blend of thinking and mumbling a few of the words to herself. Let's modify that dialog with bold text denoting the words she utters incomprehensibly:

> "I can see the hold two feet above the next draw is definitely **good** enough to **clip from**. I'd really like to clip it three moves before that, but I'm not sure that hold is positive enough. So what I'll do is hit that **sloper** and **immediately** decide if it's good enough. I'm **not** going to spend more than a **half second** making that decision. If it's not positive, I'm **going to the big locker** crimp above the bolt and clip from my waist. The fall is **safe**, and it's really not much longer if I fall from the higher hold."

It's not essential for the words to make sense to anyone. The important part is that you *say* them to animate more neurons to the cause. Highly analytical mental processes such as beta scripting enlist the slower System 2 brain—this thinking benefits from time. By *literally* talking to ourselves, we foster the mental processes best suited for deriving a concrete set of steps. Saying keywords as you ruminate through your script slows you down, which helps lodge the blueprint in your brain.

Frequently, when on-sight climbing, intra-route pause stances aren't good enough for full-blown narratives like those described above. They are either too short or too strenuous to allow enough mental bandwidth for a blow-by-blow breakdown of a sequence with alternatives. You have instead just enough time and resource to glance up-route, taking in the briefest of impressions. In these cases, you can still help yourself by quickly identifying your best-guess and using the pinpoint gaze to take in as much information as you can with the, say, half-second available. While this laser focus on one or two holds isn't as helpful as a longer narrative, it's certainly better than nothing. By directing your attention to a key few targets with your eyes via the pinpoint gaze, you help organize your intuition so that it knows where to direct its efforts in the background. Gathering just this little bit more detail helps root those holds as landmarks when you start to pull through them down the road. However, be careful to stay fully in the climbing mode at strenuous pauses. The rest isn't good enough for the full-blown analysis of System 2. What's available is a couple of purposeful glances, then you are off. Don't allow this quick plan sketching tactic to devolve into an energy-draining quagmire of analysis-paralysis.

## ***Redpoint recall***

Redpoint climbing is an evolving blend of movement *discovery* and *recall*. Early in the process, as you become familiar with the route, you are *discovering* the best sequences and potential pause stances. As you try again, you start to solidify beta scripts. Typically, these scripts nail down the hardest part of the route, leaving the more manageable parts for you to fill in as you go. We will investigate linking the little chunks of beta scripts together into a *chain* later in this chapter. For now, note the sliding scale of the redpoint process where you use pauses early in the ascent attempts to *discover*, and later as your ascents get close to finishing the route, on *recall*. In the middle, it's a blend between the two. It's a particular sort of skill to both *explore* new moves while also *remembering* to execute steps you figured out previously.

The previous example where Maya composed a beta script for the hard three-crimp crux is an example of *recall* while attempting to finish a project. Maya used her eyes directed to the foot block to recall that bit of beta, refreshing it in her mind, so it's close at hand when she needs it. Additionally, she also drafted a mnemonic, "one, two, three, foot, foot," to remember the sequence. These two techniques, locking in with the eyes and devising a simple mnemonic, assist recall. If the pause stance affords it, a fully-detailed visualization of the scheme is the best way to ensure your beta remains top of mind. Even better, running through it more than once as lucidly as possible helps grease the skids for the movement to come.

Climbers tend to be better at either discovery or recall, though there are some particularly well-suited in the middle ground. It's a good practice to identify what sort of climber you think yourself and practice the *other* kind of mentality to improve this weakness. For example, analytic climbers tend to find creating high-quality beta scripts second hat, but when they make a mistake in their plan, or can't recall how to negotiate a move they've done successfully before, they don't easily switch back over to the intuitive mode, *discovering* a way through. Spending time practicing redpoints without trying too much to remember the beta and instead treating them as on-sights again with a hint of a devil-may-care attitude may help them bring the intuitive self to the fore.

On the other hand, climbers in the intuitive camp tend to climb with a sort of amnesia, as if previous attempts didn't occur. Their beta scripts are skimpy, incomplete, and jettisoned at the first sign of a problem. This sort could help their climbing in the long term by buckling down for a few redpoint projects, practicing the creation and then flawless execution of their plan.

## Rehabilitating on the fly

Devising a script, then recalling it correctly is certainly fallible. With on-sight climbing, your blueprint is sometimes at variance with reality. Reading routes is a skill where you draw from your memory of moves you've made in the past, attempting to match them to what the arrangement of holds looks like to you from below. It's a near certainty that your prognostications won't always pan out with the infinite varieties of moves out there.

On the other hand, even with perfect redpoint scripts you've climbed through several times, you can find yourself flubbing a step and thus unmoored from your intricate procedure. In these instances, with the plan your analytical forebrain devised out the window, quickly switching to the crafty intuitive self is your only option. Robust plans hone the mind to a singular purpose, but if we find that purpose in error, we want to abandon it quickly, switching on creativity to fill the gap.

With a quick smile and perhaps a short quip, "now you've done it!", quickly engage in a meta-skill to prod yourself over to intuition. Research suggests that a good mood "affects the operation of System 1: when we are uncomfortable and unhappy, we lose touch with our intuition...A happy mood loosens the control of System 2 over performance: when in a good mood, people become more intuitive and more creative."[2] It appears that small gestures such as smiling or joking to yourself activate the very sort of mental mode required when we need to wing it.

As an example of a climber quickly changing from following a beta script to making it up on the spot, Tyrone, climbing on-sight, discovers the next two-finger pocket isn't anywhere as positive as he planned for from the ground. He responds to the harsh reality with a nice strong *wha* breath, the sides of his mouth turning into a smile while he quickly looks around for

---

[2]*Kahneman, Daniel, Thinking Fast and Slow (New York: FSG 2011) p. 44.*

an option he didn't notice earlier. Tyrone's little smile helps promote System 1's intuition. After the exhale, finding no better choice, he commits fully to the worse-than-expected pocket, enlisting a *cha* breath to help facilitate the hard pocket pull. The meta-skill of the breaths and the smile to himself in this instance help him transition from the paint-by-numbers analytical mentality. He switches from following his provisional beta, to intuiting the best solution with little input from the analytical mind.

Even better, Tyrone, after completing the route and lowering to the ground, talks this worse-than-expected pocket revelation out with Maya, demonstrating the use of *reflection*, analyzing the outcome with System 2:

**Maya**: Nice pulling it together there at that pocket. Was it not very good? It looks like a sinker from here.

**Tyrone**: Yeah, that surprised me. I was planning to clip from there, but as it turned out, I could barely pull it at all. I was lucky not to fall.

**Maya**: You didn't look like you were close to falling to me.

**Tyrone**: As soon as I woke up to the reality that the pocket was really a sloping dish, I took a flowing breath to let that anxiety out, which helped. I was like " oops! oh well!"

**Maya**: I heard that exhale. You looked pretty collected.

**Tyrone**: That's nice to hear, 'cos I'm not going to lie: I puckered a bit as I committed to pulling the pocket.

**Maya**: Did you have a plan B there?

**Tyrone**: Nope. Should have. Looking at it from the ground now, there are hints that the hold isn't very good. Look at all the chalk on tiny edges all over around that hold. That should have tipped me off that lots of people were trying to work around the pocket.

**Maya**: Now that you mention it, I see what you mean. I didn't pick up on that either.

**Tyrone**: I'm going to keep that in mind for the future. I need to take care to look closer at the route from the ground for tip-offs like that, particularly when I can get a good look at it like in this case. Then

I can at least plan for bucking up and pulling the bad hold instead of having to waste a few seconds pulling myself back together after the shock of discovery.

Tyrone becomes just a bit more wise at formulating beta scripts for future on-sight attempts as he talks out his consternation at the not-so-good pocket.

## Beta chain assemblies

*Chains* are full assemblies of climbing and non-climbing skills seamlessly linked together. Here we splice climbing movements with other tasks such as body scans or the meta-skills of the eyes and breath. In this fashion, we form an unbroken string, assembling a fully detailed set of skills for the entire route which engross and captivate the mind.

For our purposes, where the domain of the beta *script* encapsulates climbing movements through shorter sequences of about seven or shorter moves. We assemble a *chain* of perhaps multiple beta scripts, with all of the other time taken up by intuitive movement in the moment or through the execution of the skills previously described in this book. As an example, take the previous on-sight where Maya concocted a plan before a series of slopers. This beta script zeroed in on a one-bolt long series of moves. What about the rest of the route? That's where the chain comes to play.

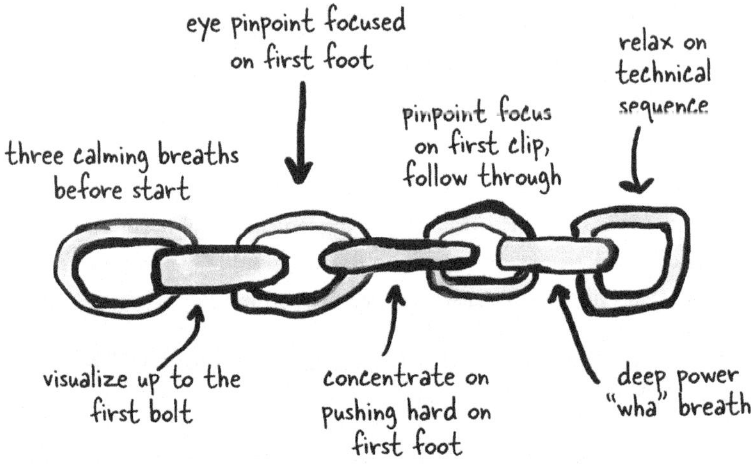


Fig 1: chaining together skills on a redpoint attempt

Instead of viewing a climb as a single task from leaving the ground to clipping the anchor, see it as a linked chain of small tasks. This makes the job of ascending the route easier to mentally digest and manage. **Figure 1** depicts a snippet of a chain from a redpoint by Tyrone. It exemplifies a chain of specific mechanics or skills assembled into one. This chain is thus a linkage of all the beta he has and the blank spaces in between. How this chain assembles is dependent on the ascent style. For some long-term redpoints, your assembled chain will contain minute detail including specific uses of your eyes and breath for nearly every single moment of the route. It's almost as detailed for the entirety of the line as a beta script. When climbing on-sight, you may be able to glean enough information from the ground to concoct a beta script or three, but most of the chain assembles while you ascend.

Let's look briefly at the chain of skills assembled by Tyrone while he works his project. The snippet in **figure 1** is just one part of it. He's ascended this particular thirty-meter climb six times previously and now has a well-formed set of beta through the crux at mid-height. The climbing before this is not very difficult, so he's spent a lot of time polishing his beta script on the crux, leaving the moves before and after this three-bolt section relatively unpracticed. We see in the illustration the segment of chain starting the three-bolt crux. Note that the chain continues on either side when he's climbing.

At the rest jug below the hard section, Tyrone starts the chain of beta illustrated in **figure 1**. This illustration details this beta chain down to the use of his eyes and the breath. This unbroken set of tasks is initiated by focusing on calming and relaxing breaths and visualization, then the physical moves begin by Tyrone mindfully approaching the first foot placement as a way to "prime the pump" for remaining attentive to the lower body through the whole ascent. He then focuses on each link, in turn, moving from link to link without pause.

While it's easier to describe how you would assemble a mental chain of skills in a redpoint ascent, since you know the moves already, it is equally applicable during on-sight attempts (**figure 2**, next page). Of course, you aren't going to know all the links beforehand. Mostly, you will *find* yourself at a specific mechanic, such as a better-than-expected rest. Finding yourself there, then making the correct decision regarding how to spend that time, then fully engaging in that skill, creates the chain on the fly. With on-sights,

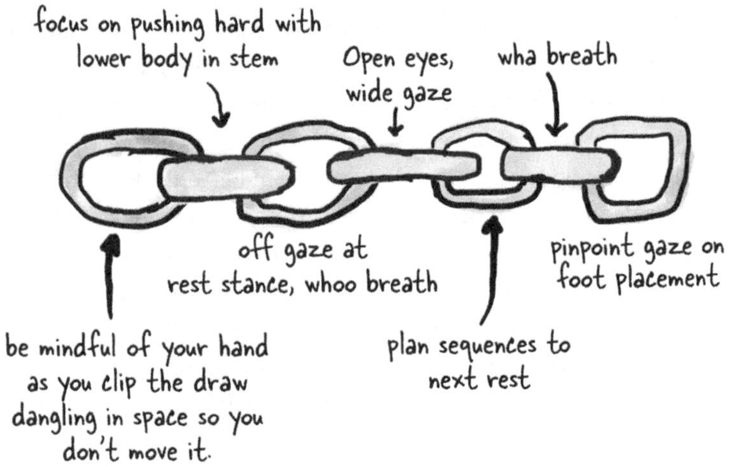


Fig 2: assembling skills during an on-sight attempt

you are more *reacting* to events, quickly and decisively choosing what skill link to add to the chain. Work to fill all moments with an actionable skill. If you find yourself without one, pick a breathing skill like a *wha*.

In both cases, redpoint and on-sight, the maxim is the same: decisively act on the task at hand. If it is resting, give yourself exclusively to maximizing that rest. If it's clipping, give full attention to the mechanic of clipping the bolt. Your eyes and breath are great choreographers of these transitions. You bring your eye focus narrow to the nose of the draw, for example, or, say, at a rest spot, you close your eyes and concentrate on a full relaxing *whoo* exhale. Next, opening your eyes with a *wide* gaze, you take in your surroundings during this on-sight attempt, helping inform your next few sequences.

There should be no idle times when climbing. Resting is a skill-based task. Planning or recalling your next sequence is a task. Each moment during a climb is an opportunity to engage fully in a skill, whatever that skill is. By using every moment with intention, you engage the climb with efficacy and craft. Even the easiest of warm-ups are a chance to engage skills mindfully. Perhaps your first route of the day will focus intently on clipping, or locking in the core, or being particularly mindful of pulling in with your hip flexors. Perhaps you will set the goal on this first easy route to stay cognizant of the *chain itself*, so you transition immediately from skill to skill with no mind wandering or delay.

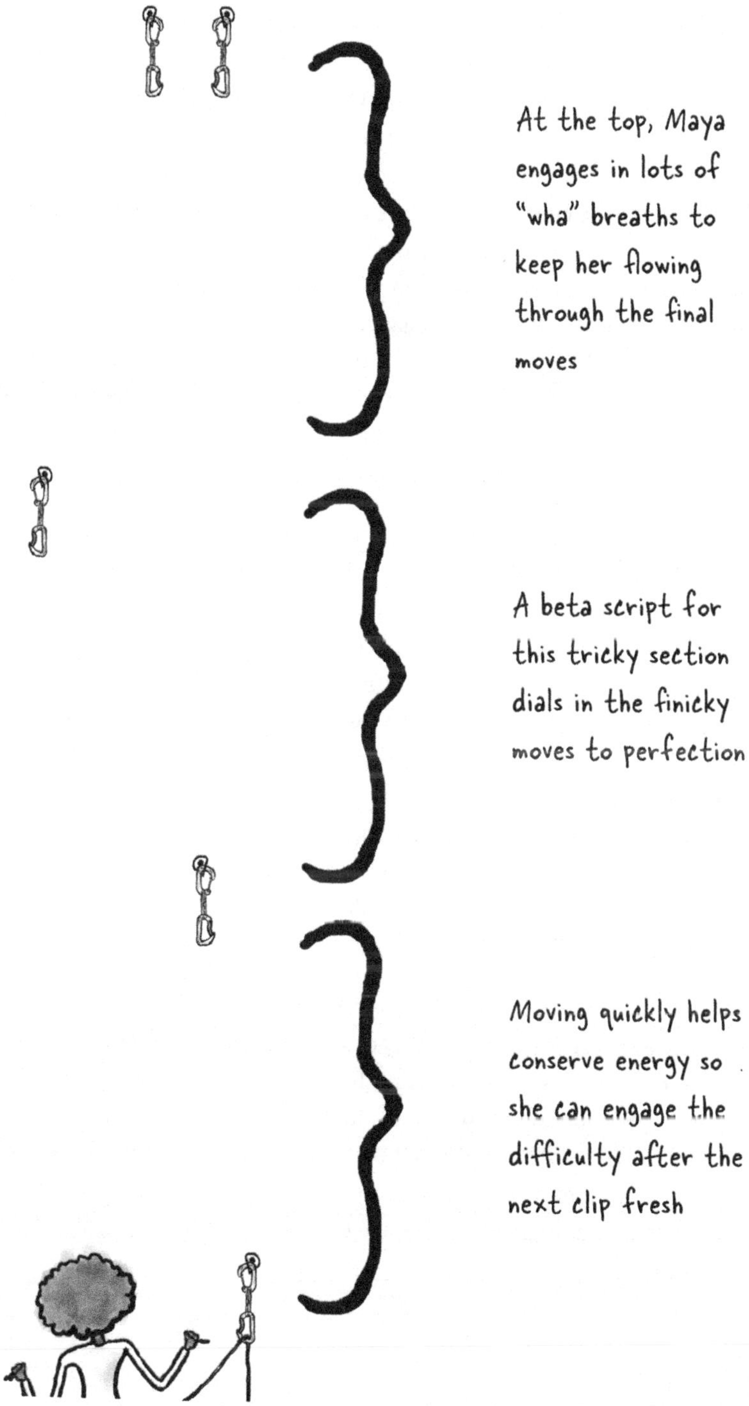
At the top, Maya engages in lots of "wha" breaths to keep her flowing through the final moves
A beta script for this tricky section dials in the finicky moves to perfection
Moving quickly helps conserve energy so she can engage the difficulty after the next clip fresh

## *Example: a snippet of a chain*

Let's turn to Maya on a redpoint attempt to illustrate an example of assembling a chain on the fly, showing how the skills described in this book link together with beta scripts. We find her on her fourth attempt, stressed out due to a combination of physical exhaustion and subjective fear, just three feet above her last bolt. She knows a few sections well, but others remain fuzzy. As she continues towards the top, her stress increases, causing her to subconsciously ditch her previous skill training. She then reverts to her most familiar movements, even when they are sub-optimal. This happens to everyone at some point, regardless of ability level. We practice skills to *procrastinate* being overwhelmed by stress. We can't eliminate stress entirely. But just because the quick and decisive alternation between skills is not a permanent fix doesn't mean it's not valuable. Small, marginal improvements result in meaningful progress.

Say she continues a few bolts at which point she encounters mental difficulties, resulting in fumbled movements and stalling out even when she knows what move to execute next. Luckily, she reaches a serendipitous rest stance she forgot about just as she starts to lose it, where she remembers to engage in a de-stressing *rag doll*. With her eyes closed, she feels the stress drip away from her as she exhales slowly. By applying this rest skill she's practiced many times, Maya brings herself back to center. She calms her rattled psyche considerably while also de-pumping her forearms. By the end of this rest, her breath returns to an even, deep, and calm state, reflecting her inner self. She started to lose track of the tightly linked chain, but with this rest, she's now able to compose herself, rededicating to the quick application of skill after skill

Continuing to track Maya's progress after this rest, we see that she opens her eyes, feeling considerably calmer. She then applies the tight eye focus of the *pinpoint* gaze to the right foot micro-edge she will use right after this rest. She focuses with her eyes intently on this tiny edge as she carefully places the toe of her right foot on it, remaining focused on that toe as she starts to weight it. With a large, powerful *wha* breath, she reaches up with her left hand to forcefully engage the route with gusto as she pulls up out of the rest.

Splicing these three skills together—the deep rest, followed by a precisely directed foot placement, then concluded with a powerful *wha* breath—serves to pull Maya from the brink of failure. This chaining of three skills marshals the mind towards movement and out of the land of mental pitfalls. After collecting herself with these specific skills, she continues to assemble the fine-grained, continuous chain of skills.

It's important to note that she didn't try to combat her brain directly with statements like "quit being scared." Instead, she reaches into her practiced quiver of skills, focusing on each in turn: it's an indirect approach to fear reduction. She doesn't focus on the fear; she focuses on the immediate task at hand.

# Chapter Six Summary

- Beta *scripts* get us through short sections. They make things easier on the mind.
- Recall your script as vividly as you can as close to when you need it.
- Beta *chains* are an assemblage of beta scripts and meta-skills, so there are no moments in ascent not engaged skillfully.
- Redpointing is an exercise in beta *recall*, on-sighting in *discovery.*
- Link meta-skills and worked-out beta script together into a seamless chain.

# Chapter 7 - Practice

Generally, sport divides time between *practice* and *performance.* In basketball, for example, players work on the fundamentals of different kinds of shots: jump-shots, free-throws, hooks, or lay-ups. They practice individual defensive skills such as running backward, or how to move around screens. These particular skills are worked together into tactics: how to handle pick-and-roll sets when defending; how to attack the weakest individual defender. In both cases, during practice, these skills are broken down into their sub-parts so a player can study and drill the mechanics at a low level. A jump shooter may practice just catching the ball, or setting their feet and squaring to the basket. As they gain mastery at these subcomponents, they then combine them into more complete skills.

They call upon this practice at comparatively uncommon game times. After games, hordes of staff on professional teams analyze the individual player's performance, talking through issues to correct with the player. These issues are broken down into skills to improve through practice. The player works with assistant coaches to enhance those skills in-season, and the player often gives particular emphasis to targeting their game's most glaring weaknesses off-season. During this off-season, the player typically undergoes a strength regimen to improve the weaknesses in their body as well. During the season, the average starting player in the NBA may play something in the range of 20 minutes a game, 82 games a year for a total *performance* of 1,640 minutes or a little over 27 hours a year. The time spent *practicing* is easily an order of magnitude higher. They practice considerably more than they perform.

While it's a false equivalence to compare a starting player in the NBA to the average climbing enthusiast, there are some important points we can draw from the comparison. The time ratio the average serious climber spends performing versus practicing is reversed: *performing* more than *practicing* if we define what *performance* means correctly. Consider *performance* climbing primarily to complete a route from bottom to top (or as far as we can, full stop) with the goal of not falling. In this mode, we aren't stopping three moves into a route because our foot placement could be better—we ignore the distant biofeedback from our foot that the placement is sub-optimal because the goal is to 'finish' the route: we are *performing.* This is the vast majority if not the *only* mode of climbing most engage. "Warming up" is merely performing on easier routes. The goal is still to ascend it without falling or stopping. Honing the craft of climbing by breaking down skills to sub-components, and practicing them in isolation is not at all common. Generally, we all could do with a lot more time spent in the practice mindset.

## When to practice

Regular, consistent practice, regardless of your ability level, hones skills. While you may find times where you allot full climbing sessions to specific proficiencies, such as a sportclimber spending a few days on easy trad routes buffing their gear-placement ability, this specially partitioned time is buttressed by a more regular routine. It's really easy to put off practice to some time in the future where you will knuckle down and finally work on technique. It's rare for that day actually to materialize. It's more realistic and easier to begin by adding little bits of practice every week, ideally to every session.

PRACTICE

The next time you climb, pick one practice drill to focus on during your warm-ups. Tell your partner if applicable of your intent before starting up the climb. Strive to engage the drill mindfully. The primary goal of the ascent is perfectly executing the drill. Successfully completing the climb is secondary.

Therefore, start the majority of your climbing sessions by picking a skill to focus on practicing, such as using your eyes or consciously engaging System 2 thinking to write great beta scripts. On the first few easy routes during your warm-up stay focused on that skill. Ideally, if you encounter a rough patch with that skill, you stop climbing and re-work the sequence to figure out the difficulty, resolving it. The most important aspect is full dedication and attention to that skill for those first few routes. Through this consistent practice, you continue to plow the groove deep into your subconscious regarding how to act. This makes the skill in question that much more available when exhausted or afraid.

Most practice occurs during your warm-ups, but sometimes you need the stress of harder climbing to engage some skills fully. The *cha* breath is an example of this need for difficulty, as without harder movement, the *cha* becomes artificial. Moreover, as you improve, you will need to add stresses (physical or mental) to keep the challenge level right in that Goldilocks zone: not too easy, not too hard, but just right. Practice allows us to learn new skills in a non-stressful environment. We then apply small increments of stress to turn the new skill into one that is battle-tested and available to us during performances. With the skill drills presented here, you may pick some nuance to focus intensely on for your first route or two of the day, then work another skill on more medium-hard routes to stress-test them. Perhaps you use the first burn on your hard route of the session as a way to target a skill, making that extra mental effort at a place you know challenges your skill ability.

Injuries are part of the sport. While a regrettable curse, they also present a great time to work on your weaker skills. Most injuries begin rehabilitation with a decreased load on your body: you climb routes well below your physical capacity to grant the injury enough stimulus to promote healing and re-strengthening, but not too much as to overly strain the rebuilding tissue. Since you aren't climbing to your standard capacity anyhow, you can focus on your rough spots. This at once helps you improve a deficient aspect of your climbing while also making your injury less burdensome. You find yourself granted time to work on a skill-set you want to advance. It partially transforms the injury into an opportunity to practice and grow. Use it as an excuse to yourself to slow down and focus on a weak area, which is difficult to do otherwise.

As an example, I once fell victim to synovitis (joint pain and swelling) in my fingers from too much crimping and inadequate warm-up (and, I suppose, just plain getting old). After taking a week off, I returned slowly to climbing by decreasing the volume and intensity of my session, focusing on my open-hand technique while eliminating crimps. After just a few sessions, I noted a significant improvement in my confidence and strength with open-handed grips, even while my synovitis symptoms subsided. Taking the time to focus this open-handed technique improved my climbing skill-base even while recovering from injury. Even after the symptoms decreased, I found that I didn't want to return to my old standard "crimp-first" approach. I continued to climb exclusively open-handed, growing in confidence and strength at that joint-angle all the while. Though I wasn't as capable or strong in total as if I allowed myself the full palette of grips, the transformation in my climbing made up for the temporary decrease. It helped migrate a weakness in my skill set to a strength. Open hand climbing is my preferred style today.

> Injury rehabilitation is a great time to work on skills.

Another time to focus on skill building is when you find yourself not up to your regular self. Perhaps a tough spat at work, recovering from a cold, exhaustion from other sports, etc., leaves your body simply unable to give you much. In these times, changing the mode from one that seeks to execute more difficult routes to one polishing skills on easier lines grants your body the recovery it needs while also helping sharpen your skill base.

## *Three kinds of knowledge*

Climbing benefits from three different levels of knowledge:[1]

1. **Indirect, learned, "third hand" knowledge**. This is the sort of knowledge that can be read in books or transmitted in the classroom. It often serves as a jumping-off point for the other two forms of knowledge as it is the most superficial, unprocessed sort, such as a simple fact like "America was discovered in 1492." Reading this book is an example of third-hand knowledge.

2. **Reflective knowledge** is the sort of learning that takes place as you ponder and digest third-hand or sensory information. You use your experience, reason, and principles to distill information into reflective knowledge. Thinking the data from this book through, and bringing your own life experiences, as well as talking about it with others is an example of reflective knowledge. With this process, you start to synthesize facts into tactics for action for yourself.

3. **Direct knowledge**. This is first-hand experience with sensory or conceptual cultivation. We often experience climbing in this direct form—many climbers (including many elite climbers) have little to no knowledge of climbing from the previous two ways of knowing. Asked about how they overcome various obstacles (mentally, physi-

---

[1] *Bhikkhu, Budhadasa, Under the Bodhi Tree (Somerville: Wisdom Publications, 2017), p.22*

cally, or technically), those with exclusively *direct* knowledge won't be able to answer. They *know* the answer, but only directly in their bones. It hasn't been articulated upwards or conveyed into the other two sorts of knowledge. Practicing the concepts from this book helps bake them into direct knowledge.

For climbing, like any sport, we ultimately want this third type of knowing. The other two are rarely helpful in ascent. However, we can't transmit direct knowledge from one person to another. For me to communicate a direct insight into climbing that would help you, I must convert my direct experience (number three in the previous list) to indirect (number one). This would likely require me to engage reflectively (the second) to come up with words that accurately depict my direct understanding.

The recipient then must take these words and work them back down to direct knowledge in him or herself. It's not enough to read the words. Unlike learning a list of facts, you can't *learn* to climb through the third-hand approach, though it's often a great place to start. You must use reflection to digest book-learning into direct knowledge through practice. Practice bakes the concepts into your muscles, resulting in direct knowledge. Even better, practice mixed with reflective knowledge results in direct knowledge of the initial third-hand information, along with subtleties you might discover for yourself–you take ownership. So while you practice the concepts in this book or elsewhere, use your System 2 mind to turn them into your own by challenging and extending them.

Another way of looking at this is that you dedicate yourself to getting your *mind into your muscles*. While practicing, we focus on a concept such as exploring pinpointing your feet, using practice ascents as a means to turn the indirect knowledge into direct knowledge. You get more out of a drill the more you keep your attention on it, instead of just going through the motions on autopilot.

As an example, say Kai wants to see how he might improve his climbing through the use of the breath by playing around with the material from **Chapter 3**. He's particularly interested in exploring the differences between the *wha* and the *cha* breath, and when it seems better to use one over the other. Kai knows he's easily distracted by others climbing around him, so he opts to come into the gym early on a Sunday morning when no one is around so he can practice these two styles of breathing with his partner.

After warming up, he finds a moderately strenuous climb with a multiple move crimping crux that he thinks he can repeat several times. This sequence is strenuous enough so that breathing doesn't feel contrived, but not so difficult that his mind can't cope with the climbing. This allows him to focus on his breath.

He attempts the crux sequence several times that session with the only goal to focus on using either the *wha* or the *cha* breath. When he makes it through that section, he lowers to the ground, even though there are fifteen feet left to go. Kai doesn't care about completing the climb as much as about learning more about how these two breathing styles might help his climbing. Lowering immediately after the "experiment" helps him both by saving his strength for the next attempt and by keeping that crux move top of mind so that he can recall it easily and reflect on the breathing.

Back on the ground, Kai immediately reflects on the crux sequence, evaluating his first try. He talks it through with his belayer, Ichero:

> **Kai**: Well, that attempt was a bit awkward. I was thinking a lot about the *cha* breath and stalled out on the crimps.
>
> **Ichero**: I noticed the first one seemed slow, but I clearly heard you push the breath out after you hit that first crimp, so that's good.
>
> **Kai**: I don't even recall that. I remember thinking about how tight my chest felt, but I don't remember the first exhale.
>
> **Ichero**: It was clear to me. It sounded just like it was described in the book.
>
> **Kai**: Cool, I'm glad you were paying attention. With the difficulty of the move and the newness of that breath style, my brain apparently couldn't take it all in.
>
> **Ichero**: I also noticed that the next two cha's were not as explosive on the exhale—
>
> **Kai**: That's funny. I actually remember semi-consciously telling myself to explode the breath out there. It's interesting that when I wasn't so attentive, I seemed to exhale more forcefully.

**Ichero**: It's not that surprising to me that you are all over the map as I've never heard you exhale at all while climbing. It makes a lot of sense to me. It's new.

**Kai**: I guess so. OK, in a minute after I've recovered, I'm going to do the same thing again, but this time I'm going to pay close attention to that first *cha* exhale.

Reflecting on his performance with Ichero, Kai starts to take a concept—in this case the *cha* breath—and, through conscious thought, train his subconscious how to use this skill: he takes his mind into his muscles. Kai doesn't have a lot of mental bandwidth at the moment while climbing to process the breathing skill. Reflecting on how it went, and talking it out with Ichero, helps him unravel the attempt. He uses this information to inform his next try, building direct knowledge of the *cha* breath.

# Some Practice Guidelines

The process of development and growth is multifaceted and complex. The following list outlines a few hallmarks of progression. In the context of improving our craft, we can use the following as a general rubric. This list is agnostic to skill level. It could be applied to help a climber advance in nominal grades or to gain a stronger sense of self-efficacy.

- **Become less narrow-minded of the possible options for improvement.** Opportunities for growth often occur through the improvement of aspects other than physical strength. If you find yourself dangling from the rope, remember to start asking yourself questions about how you could have been more effective or skillful with your movements to *save* your muscles instead of blaming your lack of strength for the failure.

- **Get interested in ways that you could improve.** It will often take some time to figure out what mechanics or behaviors you must develop to progress. Ask yourself "what if" questions—"What if I pushed harder with my foot on that sloper I don't trust? Would that help?" Here are a few examples of things a climber may see in themselves:

*- I notice other climbers flag their feet and back-step in places I never do. I want to adopt some of that style in my climbing*

*- I seldom move dynamically! I want to practice not climbing statically, moving with more momentum and speed.*

*- I've been procrastinating including practice falls as a regular part of my climbing session. What if I start doing those now?*

- **Set goals around those areas.** Realistic goals are not easy. Most goals must be broken down into sub-goals that are actionable and measurable to satisfy your inner sense of making it. Goals too large are tantamount to wishful thinking. "I will work on focusing on getting more 'push' out of holds I don't trust on this next attempt" is more actionable than "I should improve my technique." Be specific with concrete actions you can undertake in the short term.
- **Commit to the goal.** This requires dedicated practice of the skill in question isolated from other concerns, with patience and a realistic sense of the amount of time needed to see improvements. If you determine fat loss is a top goal, the quantity of time to see improvements takes months. Or, as another example, learning to allow more weight to transfer to your feet takes a little time and continuous effort.
- **Automate them.** "A great deal of training in sports is undertaken precisely to circumvent the limitations of the slow, effortful Type 2 processing and automate behaviors."[2] Through the practice of skills, we migrate them from System 2 to 1. This move to System 1 eases the cognitive load of that skill, freeing the mind for other tasks.

Overall ability improves through the practice of rudimentary skills in non-performance settings, or, in other words, where you have manageable stress. This allows you to slow down and focus on the skill instead of the other aspects of climbing. While, in basketball, there is a lot known about how to improve the jump-shot, with climbing, comparatively little is known about even what specific skills to train, let alone how actually to go about practicing them.

---

[2]*Furley, p. 3*

If we identify sequences during performances that seem foreign, then we've identified an opportunity to create a drill to level up that particular aspect, so it's more game-time worthy. Put another way, practicing the minute elements of climbing movements takes on a life of its own. As you learn more about the details of specific mechanics during practice, these details add a new dimension: it's no longer merely a clip, but a sequence of movements, each of which requires attention, each of which you have finely honed in practice.

When starting the practice of a skill, use the most 'natural' and stress-free environment. For most climbers, this means easy gym routes. However, if you are practicing in the gym, find the time when you are outdoors on a stress-free route to concentrate on the basics of a given skill as well. Many gym climbers have a tough time transitioning to real rock: applying the same tactic of slowing down in a stress-free environment outdoors can help. Spending a whole day climbing trivial routes at the start of the season is another way to help stepping off of plastic and onto stone.

## *The Goldilocks principle: crawl, walk, run*

To improve, we need to stay in the channel between too hard and too easy—the Goldilocks zone. Many climbers start too hard, triggering anxiety. This is easy to do when returning to fundamental skills such as clipping. There's a lot of value to breaking down a skill to rudiments, practicing those rudiments at a low-stress level, then continuing to practice just that single mechanic under increasing stress as you improve. So, for example, if you find yourself not pulling up rope fluidly, run a drill on the easiest terrain you can find so you can concentrate fully on that mechanic. This gives you a lot of analytic firepower to use on that single aspect of the clip. You can figure out in what situations that fluidity is problematic and address it in a low/no stress environment.

You could look at this as the *crawl* stage in a three step process of *crawl, walk*, then *run*. Many either skip the crawl entirely or fail to give it due consideration. Moreover, even when you reach elite status on a skill, you can still learn by returning to the crawl stage from time to time as you discover some small variant on a skill that is troublesome. This is a great time to engage the slow and effortful System 2 thinking. Ask yourself "what if" questions and think through movements you usually gloss over.

Learning new skills takes time. You can sometimes regress as you replace your old methods and mechanics. You need to give yourself the time and space to allow the new skill to replace the old. Practicing a specific skill can also become a reward in itself. For example, I find it very rewarding on my first warm-up route of the day to accomplish a clipping drill with 100% accuracy. Feeling the efficacy of pulling up the rope flawlessly, focusing on the nose of the draw, and clipping it clean every time with speed is not easy. I'm also a harsh judge—the slightest bobble "subtracts points" in my personal tally, or I'll ding my score if I fail to follow through fully with my eyes. With the deliberate increased difficulty due to these strict rules, even the first route of the day becomes a rewarding challenge itself.

In this example, notice as well that we are breaking down a larger mechanic of clipping into sub-components. One is the act of pulling up the rope. You may find that this isn't atomic enough either. After all, it is a compound movement in itself, requiring a coordinated effort of many thought processes and muscle groups. Perhaps you need to break it down even further as you start to identify in the crawling stage what *exactly* is causing the difficulty. Maybe you find that you fumble finding the rope if you aren't looking at it. Perhaps during this analysis, you discover that the problem is that your knot isn't tied close enough to your harness, leaving a big rats' nest of rope right where your hand wants to grab it. Tying a cleaner knot may be a way to resolve this. *Crawling* is a time where you are going slow enough where things like this tend to reveal themselves. The additional bandwidth available when the climbing is more comfortable allows consciousness room to detect these issues.

Alternatively, perhaps you could try simply roping up and making one move onto an easy route, then finding the rope at your harness without looking at it. Doing that several times with each hand could then help you progress more than upping the ante by climbing an easy route to simply locate the rope blindly the whole way up. You first *identify the problem*, then come up with a drill that you can do in the *least stressful environment* where you can succeed reliably at the skill without encountering the problem you discovered. When you can successfully crawl, then start adding small bits of stress to increase your ability to begin entering the walk phase.

As your skills improve, you must increase the difficulty to remain engaged. There's a sweet spot for a given ability level at somewhere around a 50% success rate where the motivation is highest. You are challenged enough by this difficulty level to engage but not so much as to become debilitatingly anxious. As your skills increase, the challenge must as well. In climbing, this challenge typically denotes an increase in grade, but it could (and should) also be working at skills at which you are comparatively weak. Perhaps you would find it sufficiently challenging to clip on overhanging terrain as you find both the climbing and the clipping considerably more stressful than when on up-to-vertical rock. Or perhaps you want to improve your traditional climbing and thus spend weeks on routes many grades below your sport climbing expertise as you grow in your ability in that realm.

To reiterate an important point, during the *crawl* stage, it's a good idea to go slower than usual and exaggerate the movement. As you progress to *walking*, you start to add stresses to the skill. The pressure could be mental, physical, or technical, but you need to be careful about adding too much too quickly—keep the Goldilocks principle in mind: if you add too much challenge too soon, you slow your progression at best, and stunt development at worst. As an extreme example, say a climber fumbles foot placements on overhanging terrain. She decides to work on that, breaking down the mechanics and discovering that she never pinpoints her feet in these situations. This climber designs a drill for herself: on top-rope, she rests before starting the steep section she chose on a gym route. While resting, she reminds herself that above all else she will keep eye contact precisely on the footholds to the next bolt.

She crawls this drill she made for herself on the easiest overhanging route in the gym a few times, but then, thinking she solved the problem on the stress-free 5.9 gym climb, moves to an R-rated route outside. This is far too big a jump: she went from *crawl* to *run*. A better transition would be moving up a grade or two in the gym where the stress of safety is not a concern, but the stress of the climbing ups the ante just a bit. Another possible progression would be something like doing those moderate routes at the end of a session when she's tired, or not resting on the rope before the overhang. While you want to crawl while fresh mentally and physically, as you continue to stress-proof your tactic, doing it when you aren't fresh mentally or physically (provided, of course, you are ready for that challenge increase) is a great way to make progress towards the run level. This helps prepare the proficiency for true performances like a goal route.

A way to envision this is a pyramid with lots of low and slow stuff at the base topped with the dynamic, momentum-driven skill building for more advanced practice when you are ready to peak the pyramid. In the middle are tune-ups that you work on as the result of discovering issues with the skills.

## *Speed and Momentum*

*Slowing down* is ultimately not how we want to climb during performances, as vital as it is at first. As you master the drill, increasing the speed is key to incorporating the technique. We want to execute the skill in question as fast as we can *accurately* perform it. A common problem among climbers is moving far too slowly and statically during hard sections. The use of momentum and speed is one of the critical ways of gaining efficiency, but it is somewhat at odds with practice.

A way to solve this is to start slow, concentrating on the movement, then apply speed as you close down on mastery of a given skill. The key is to remain focused on accuracy even as you apply more velocity. Of course, as you up the ante by trying to execute the skill more quickly, you will start to "miss" a bit. Keep in mind the research on the *quiet eye* discussed in **Chapter 3** suggests that we need more time than seems intuitive to lock on to targets so the brain can orchestrate the muscles correctly. Don't short-change this aspect of the movement.

PRACTICE

On top rope on the easiest, juggiest gym climb you can find, practice using momentum and climbing dynamically with your hands by only using one of them. Generate 100% of your momentum using one hand. After a few moves, switch hands. Even when you think you can't make the move one-handed, give it all you can.

For example, if you are practicing the clipping drill, you may bobble them more often as you speed up. Take a few tries with this velocity then evaluate if you think you can adapt to the new speed with more practice or if it's better to slow back down. Most people move up the difficulty curve too quickly, going from *crawl* to *run*, skipping walking. They end up not running so well.

Over time as you incorporate specific drills into your climbing routine, you naturally find a normal speed. Every once in a while, like perhaps your first route of the day, slow way down, becoming mindful of the perfect execution of the mechanic. For example, on your easy first warm-up in the gym, go through the clipping drill at half-speed. Take note of how your hand naturally finds the rope and pulls it up. Study the nose of the quickdraw, noticing little details like the polish of the nose or how much it's swinging as you place your hand on it to push the rope through. Notice how your eyes want to move off the draw to their next target. Do you feel the urgency to run too fast? Is it difficult to remain focused on the mechanic?

When you move faster, you tend to do so more dynamically. Instead of discrete moves (i.e. "left hand… right foot…"), the sequences tend to blend as, for example, the fulcrum of your left hand directs the force from a hard leg push upwards to your right hand. Instead of waiting for your entire weight to land on your right hand, you use some of the remaining upwards force generated from the hard leg push to then reset your left hand higher. In this example, a three-move sequence blends into one that takes less energy than the sum of the three separately. Learning to identify ways of generating momentum by making each move a little less discrete is a great thing to practice in its own right, but often needs to be the icing on the cake. Again, accuracy first, then speed.

> Speed and Momentum are among the best ways to improve efficiency. Using momentum needs special attention and practice itself. When practicing a mechanic, make sure to practice it at an increased pace–the fastest you can accomplish accurately and smoothly.

Additionally, while practicing, we may continue to isolate specific stimuli to improve upon after we nail the basics down pat, growing increasingly nuanced. For me, some safe falls stimulate more fear with just small, odd changes. I noticed that I don't really like falling above roofs when they cut onto a headwall: I hesitate and slow, to the detriment of performance. Even if the protection is close, when I can't see the bolt down below me, it adds a measure of stress. This fear-reduction is something that I can work on in the safe confines of the gym by making an effort to practice falls on terrain that stimulate this fear.

Taking ownership of your continued development requires the cultivation of *curiosity*. As you run through the drills presented in this book, you may start to get a sense of how to identify and remedy problem spots in your climbing not explicitly noted here. As you have seen already in this book, being open to improvements in your mental and technical game instead of just focusing on strength opens doors to improvement with many avenues to exploit. As you start to identify an area for development, think about how you can break that mechanic down into sub-skills that are actionable at a crawl. For example, perhaps you will notice that on steep stone you don't maintain body tension, allowing your core to sag. What sorts of drills can you come up with to practice maintaining tension?

Let's consider an a solution to this question. Since even easy overhanging routes tend to force so much weight on the hands that it's hard to have enough time to practice comfortably before the pump makes the practice too trying. In other words, some skills are difficult to make easy enough so that it feels like crawling. Perhaps the crawl stage is going up two or three bolts so you can move slow enough to focus on body tension, back-stepping, and other odd movements typical of climbing overhangs. You want as much focus and brainpower available as possible so you can learn the mechanic before moving on to stress-proofing it. Make sure you keep it easy to start with.

As a practical matter, while I've described the *crawl, walk, run* tactic linearly, in practice, most climbers won't be quite as strict in these steps—nor do a lot of skills for a given climber require it. A lot of the time, climbers just need to back down to "early walk." In the example of concentrating on the rope pull, sometimes all that is required is just to *walk* (practice) that at an average speed during the warm-up phase of the session. Then, that rope pull mechanic remains slightly in focus just due to the priming that occurred during the warm-up.

Don't shortchange yourself, however: take the time to slow it down so you can overcome a problem in a movement. The payoff for getting truly remedial with a conscious crawling phase of a skill pays significant dividends. Often the trouble spot is just a small error in the mechanic, such as the discovery that you hold your breath after the completion of deadpoints. No matter the ability level, we all at times need to slow down to diagnose the underlying bug. You might not notice subtleties such as your breath hampering your movements when executing delicate deadpoint moves under the barrage of stimulus experienced when climbing normally, yet it is often these sort of small corrections that add up to an overall improvement in ability.

It takes solid, concentrated effort to burn in new muscle memories. Even though it may feel beneath you, the time spent crawling will take you further than applying too much stress too soon. If you can't concentrate fully on the new mechanic to replace your old, you can't start plowing in that groove that you want to fall into when stress is high. Effort and dedication can often substitute natural ability. Conscious practice can overcome physical limitations. A bullheaded attitude might provide the most essential ingredients required to clip the chains.

## Plateau or no?

It takes longer than we think for these things to bake in—as in months or years. Even with a drill as seeming one-and-done as the tight focus on clipping we've discussed, you have to spend time regularly honing the skill for the benefits to take hold reliably in stressful times, for the fine points of a skill are the first to go under pressure.

Take an exercise rather common to climbing for example: practicing lead falling[3]. Many, perhaps most, climbers have engaged in this practice. A lot of them gain a measure of improvement over the fear of falling by doing so. However, many who engage and improve in this practice do not continue it long term. While it's certainly true that we experience a diminishment in return to our investment as we continue to drill a particular skill such as this, it is also true that the smaller gains still matter. Our brain is hard-wired to remember negative experiences much more strongly than positive ones. We help inoculate ourselves from the regressive impact of the fear of falling by the continual reinforcement of positive experiences through practice.

> Skill building takes time to see results. Keep faith and continue the practice.

While more robust than muscular strength, skills atrophy without continuous practice. If you haven't been intentionally placing narrow focus on targets with the pinpoint gaze to direct attention for a while, you will likely start to slide back somewhat. Continuing to practice simple drills as part of your daily routine helps keep you sharp no matter your ability level. Moreover, focusing intentionally on skills over the long term tends to bring up ways you could improve: you start to notice subtle problems as you continue to focus strongly on the basics. Where, say, six months ago you barely had any awareness of your feet whatsoever, with continuous practice, you find increasingly subtle yet important ways you can engage them. You deepen your innate biomechanical advantage and improve your climbing efficiency.

---

[3]For details regarding the practice of lead falling, see *Ilgner, Arno, Espresso Lessons From the Rock Warrior's Way (La Vergne: Desiderata, 2009).*

Skills and strength both follow a hockey-stick shape of progression. Early in the curve, you gain a lot of ability. As you trend toward mastery, the improvements are smaller and harder to notice. With skill-building in particular, this far-right tail starts to appear like a plateau or maximum growth, so the tendency is to stop the practice: "what's the use? I've mastered it!" However, slow progression eventually leads to noticeable improvements even if proficiency benchmarks occur increasingly infrequent. By keeping the faith, you remain marching upwards, if slowly.

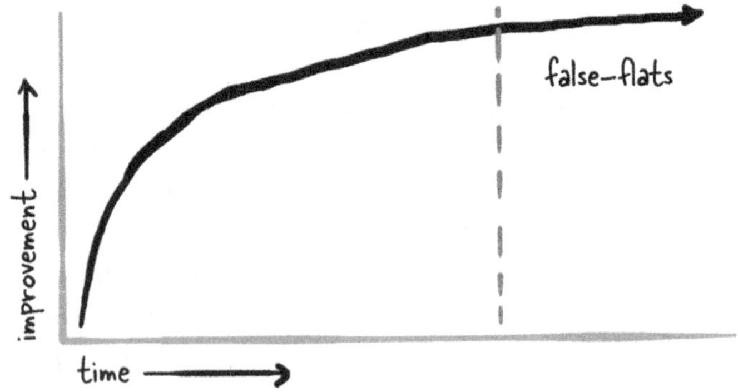


In the diagram above, the curve of improvement over time levels off. When it passes the dotted line, the climber enters the region of "false-flats." Imagine if you walked up a hill the shape of that curve. Past the dotted line, the one percent grade doesn't seem like ascending at all any more: it feels like you are on flat ground. However, since that small (and diminishing) increase continues far into the distance, over time you gain a lot of elevation if you just keep walking long enough.

With skill-building, what appears a performance plateau is nearly always a false-flat. You are improving at the skill, but the improvement is too subtle to see in the short term. It may take significant time before it results in material change. Continuing regular, mindful practice eventually results in marked gains.

Returning back to our clipping example, regular practice of this simple, hum-drum mechanic over the months and even years likely results in a slow one percent decrease in bobbled clips as you improve gradually. This means that you will miss just one or two fewer clips—and thus save perhaps a few precious seconds when it matters—for every 100, or one every few sessions. You won't likely notice this improvement, but it's real. The tiny increase in ability, when bundled with other minute skill improvements, coalesces into meaningful proficiency over time. Paired with a likewise improvement in strength, this results in a better climber.

### *There's so much to practice*

While this book focuses on the proficiencies of the eyes, breath, restoration, and lower body, this certainly isn't an exhaustive list of the all ingredients that constitute successful climbing. Tenaciousness, trying hard, and remaining positive in the face of doubt exemplify other skills that are equally deserving of practice. For some climbers–myself among them–practicing simply continuing to give it everything in the face of doubt, fiery pump, and blown beta ranks among the most important sorts of practice, as an example. *Trying hard* is a skill the improves with practice. Being honest with your weaknesses and then having the bravery to address them nearly always results in growth.

You never outgrow practice.

# Chapter Seven Summary

**Dedicated time to practicing skills pays off in the long term. Staying regular and remaining curious leads to growth.**

- Adding regular thoughtful practice to your repertoire is a great way to improve.
- Practice is not *performing*. You are working on a specific skill in relative isolation. Leave your ego at home.
- We learn best when the practice is difficult enough to engage our mind, but not so difficult that we are likely to fail.
- You have to practice regularly to get the most benefit.
- Engaging the mind and making a drill your own is the best way to internalize the ability so that it becomes intuitive.
- As you trend towards mastery of a skill, small gains take a lot longer to realize. However, these minute improvements are worth the effort.

# Chapter 8 - Craft

Many facets contribute to effective and rewarding climbing. Certainly, physical strength ranks high—if not highest—among them. Climbers rarely hone other aspects of their craft outside of strength, however, saying things like "some day, I'll really buckle down and work on slopers," but never actually staying dedicated long enough to this weak proficiency at a level easy enough to foster change. Or, as another example, the climber avoids working on the fear of falling, leaving it lurking in the shadows to the detriment of performance. This lack of purposeful engagement in skill development results in stunted techniques and mental hang-ups for which the climber must work around by pulling harder, wasting energy. He pulls harder crimp moves to avoid easier slopers, for example. This not only stifles externally visible ability, but internal pleasure and enjoyment in mastery as well.

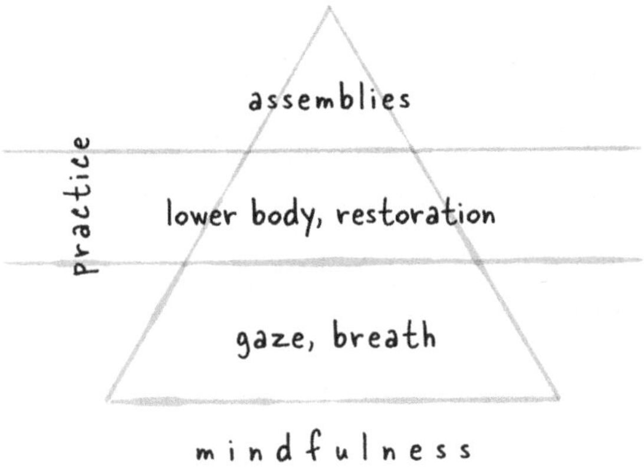


As a way to counteract this tendency, we began *Climbing Craftsmanship* with the outline of two mental models: attention/awareness and System 1/ System 2, setting the foundation for the exploration of the craft of climbing rooted in mindfulness. With knowledge of the tendencies of the mind, we encourage the helpful aspects of our hard-wiring while working around its limitations. Knowing that the mind wants to rush when under pressure, we counteract short-changing foot placement through the pinpoint gaze, for instance, triggering a positive chain reaction. Craftsmanship, in effect, strengthens us through efficient use of the resources we already have.

We also looked at the tendency of the mind to fabricate fear, sometimes with little to no objectivity. Often, climbing, particularly sport climbing, remains a safe endeavor, yet the primal fear of heights and falling forge red-hot anxieties. Centering on skills—remaining ever mindful—serves as an antidote to these anxieties. We don't want to ignore potentially legitimate, objective dangers. Instead, we want to measure risk accurately so that safe environments are less likely to evoke debilitating anxiety.

Climbers are almost always *performing*, rarely if ever *practicing*, nearly always trying to get to the top of a route without falling by any means necessary. While this is undoubtably a valid and important way of climbing, the exclusivity of this mode pushes other approaches totally out of the picture. Spending time working on skills without worrying if you accomplished all the moves without resting or falling helps you grow.

We've explored several techniques and skills in this book, but many other aspects that could help climbing deserve attention too, such as:

- **Diet**. Our body thrives with proper nutrition. Eating incessant junk calories exacts a price.
- **Fuel**. Having enough energy empowers our best efforts. Eating an impeccable diet, yet not enough of it, short-changes ability.
- **Sleep**. Climbing creates micro-tears in our muscles and supportive tissue. 95% of the hormones that initiate the rebuilding and repairing of that trauma and, hopefully, the resultant super-compensation that makes us stronger, occurs in deep sleep. You *damage* muscles training; you *build* them sleeping. The quantity, quality, and consistency of sleep is therefore a most important aspect to physical training.

These areas along with innumerable others contribute significantly both to your ability and enjoyment while climbing. Many of these areas ask you to make non-trivial changes in the outlook and habits in your life writ large. In this way, you become increasingly familiar with the needs of the body and mind, with positive spillover effects elsewhere in your life.

We explored the two *meta-skills*: the gaze and the breath. These "skills of skills" are of particular import because they are virtually always available to employ, and act quickly as a salve to anxieties, fear, and muscular exhaustion. They buttress climbing movement, helping pacify the psyche. When feeling the rise of fear, the quick employment of a meta-skill such as a *whoo* breath helps disperse this anxiety while giving the mind a task on which to focus so that it doesn't spin off into the "what if" hamster wheel.

The way we use our eyes—the *gaze*—acts as a conduit of intent. Pinpoint focus strongly marshals attention on a target to the exclusion of the remaining field of awareness, for example. Through the use of a particular gaze, we activate specific neural pathways while deactivating others, fostering a way of thinking and perceiving in alignment with our immediate goal. We reinforce what we want to happen with our body through manifesting intention through our eyes.

Breathing patterns, the second meta-skill, also shepherd specific mentalities, helping us engage the sympathetic (aroused) or parasympathetic (calm) nervous system. Additionally, the breath sets pace while prompting us to move, keeping us flowing. The regular, free, and powerful breath boosts our reserve of power. The breath at once empowers and relaxes.

The two primary restoration skills, the *rag doll* and *body scan*, are powerful mechanisms for recharging the batteries while ascending. These restorative techniques use the meta-skills of the *off* gaze and the *whoo* breath to set the stage for a nearly meditative repose that at once rejuvenates the body and mind. Growing proficiency with identification and application of restoration skills helps the climber ascend relaxed both in the muscles and the psyche. This increased skill also promotes meaningful restoration at marginal stances, assisting letting go of the past, climbing upwards without traces of these earlier difficulties dragging you down.

Your powerful lower body, which dwarfs the strength of the upper, requires specific, dedicated attention to use to maximal advantage. This is what most refer to as "technique." The alpha and omega of efficient employment of your lower body—and therefore the keystone to superior technique—is optimal foot placement. This begins with the pinpoint gaze so that the foot anchors to the stone with your full attention prior to moving on to the next task, assuring the subconscious that the big guns of the trunk are green-lit to push maximally without blowing off the hold. Pinpointing the foot is perhaps the most important way of taking pressure off the arms.

The last skill in the pyramid discussed in *Climbing Craftsmanship*, assembling bits of beta into the smaller, more tactical *scripts*, and then, ultimately into the strategic *chain*, help us, like the meta-skills, stay vigilantly on task during the ascent. These scripts and chains keep the mind busy at all times, without mindless gaps that tend to fester fear and anxiety. "Writing" and then following beta scripts appropriately matches the System 1 / System 2 mental model such that we strongly delineate action from thinking, using both to best effect. The mind reacts best to strong stimulus when a vision of the future is clear. Highly detailed beta scripts make the mind less reactive to the difficulties of climbing.

Of the skills that don't come as naturally, such as, say, following through with the eyes, we must practice in a lower-stress environment, concentrating on these foreign and easily forgettable skills to the exclusion of everything else. Additionally, learning subtleties in this mode augments the sense of accomplishment and mastery over the domain. Climbing encompasses an untold myriad of often unusual and sometimes downright bizarre ways of actuating the body. Movement pattern acquisition and practice of related skills such as the use of the eyes bakes these atypical patterns into the muscles so that they become second nature. It takes dedicated and regular practice and thoughtful analysis and self-reflection to get the most out of these patterns. Reading about it in this book or others isn't enough. You must use your mind and intuition to consciously drive them deep, so they assist you when you most need them.

Adding regular skill development such as described in this book to your routine helps round out your climbing so that other goals, such as a well breathed route climbed relaxed and calm, become rewarding goals too: climbing isn't, after all, just about achieving our hardest number. It's also about perfecting rudiments, particularly in our weakest proficiencies. When a stunted ability such as slab climbing or ascending relaxed in the body and/or calm in the mind transforms into a honed skill, the sense of mastery over the sport blossoms. Craftsmanship implies studious practice; from this, the rewards of climbing grow. Completing a more modestly graded route secure with the internal pride that you executed it with your highest degree of craft is equally as rewarding as desperately clawing your way to your hardest ascent, damn the torpedoes. Of course, the two—your hardest and your most well-executed climbs—are not mutually exclusive. When they coincide, it bestows a peak moment.

# Appendix

## Mental Model Details

In **Chapter 1**, we outlined the Attention/Awareness and System 1 and System 2 mental models. This appendix explores these modes of thinking in more detail, clarifying the concepts and how to apply them to your ascents.

### *Attention and awareness*

This first model of the mind helps us understand how our brain processes the significant stress of climbing. Armed with this knowledge, we can build skills to improve our psychology in service to our climbing goals. This model divides consciousness in two: *attention* and peripheral *awareness.*[1] What do these two terms mean?

Vision is an excellent analogy to the differences between attention and awareness. Your vision has two parts: as you read this, the macula of your eye lands on each word of the page. It's what you are conscious of actually "seeing" when vision dominates attention. Of course, you also see quite a bit more than the single word you happen to be reading at any given moment. You also vaguely take in all of the other words on the page, along with everything else in the field of vision. Perhaps someone walks by. Attention continues to focus on the printed words on the page while part also registers—is *aware* of—the movement in the background. Your visual consciousness is thus a blend of attention and awareness: in this example, you consciously *attend* to the words you are reading while also unconsciously *aware* of the person walking across the room. There are, of course, innumerable other simultaneous precepts in awareness as well: the sound of the refrigerator humming, the feeling of the chair on your back, or perhaps a sense of thirst, to enumerate a few of many.

---

[1]For more details regarding this model, see: *Yates, John, The Mind Illuminated (New York: Touchstone, 2015).*

Awareness acts in the background, monitoring that which we are not attending. Should that person who we were dimly aware of walking in the background suddenly lurch in our direction, we would unconsciously shift the object of attention from the written words on the page to this person. That would then become the focus of attention. We would then only be distantly and vaguely aware of the words written on the page. For the untrained mind, attention vacillates rapidly between many different focuses. In this example, attention quickly turns to the person who lurched in our direction, made sense of their action (say they nearly dropped something), then turned the focus back to the words on the page. Perhaps in a few sentences, we might spontaneously then turn attention to thinking about the need to remember to call mom on her birthday in a few days, then a split second later about how a cup of coffee sounds good. Then back to reading again. This exemplifies the standard, run-of-the-mill quick alternation of attention. Those thoughts seem like they are happening in the background (awareness), but, actually, attention is oscillating between several objects in turn.

Let's look at a quick example of this attention/awareness distinction in climbing. Consider a climber in a stem corner. Her right front outside foot contacts the left wall on a micro-edge. Her left foot is back-stepped into a drop-knee, smearing on the left wall. She palms into the left wall with her left hand, pushing hard. Her right hand is in an insecure finger lock in the crack at the back of the corner. She is *attentive* at the moment of the need to move her left hand from the palming stance up to the next finger lock, but also *aware* of how precarious it feels to release the tension of that left palm as it is counterbalancing the drop-knee.

Additionally, she's less aware of her feeling of thirst, her tight, restricted breathing, the hair in her eyes, and how the sun suddenly came out in full force. A remote part of her registers (is aware of) a slight uptick in fear at the precarious placement of her right foot on the micro-edge, as her subconscious equates heat and intense sunlight with reduced rubber friction. An even more remote part of her is just barely aware of her belayer chirping bland notes of encouragement from below, and the vague realization that she probably just used her last cam.

## Sub-minds

We can look at awareness as an aggregate of many *sub-minds*, each with its domain of responsibility. For example, we have the sensory sub-minds relating to vision, one for smell, hearing, etc. Then there are other sub-minds responsible for mental activities such as motor coordination. While attention starts focused on our conscious choice, over time, much like the squeakiest wheel gets the grease, the loudest sub-mind tends to "win" consciousness at any given moment. This squeaky-wheel phenomenon often results in our burning, screaming forearms grabbing consciousness from us, even if attention should operate elsewhere to achieve the goal. We may want to focus on perfectly placing our foot on that micro-crystal so we can get the most out of our lower body. Still, the sub-mind responsible for processing the neural input from our forearm steals attention away—attention magnetizes to the arms.

By climbing more mindfully, we can focus attention on the object of intention, even when a sub-mind wants to pull us away from it. As an example, we stay attentive to the careful placement of our left foot, even while our right forearm strongly demands our attention, or our internal emotions demand us to focus on the fear of falling. Practicing stable attention to our intentions is a skill that requires practice.

These two different ways of knowing, attention and awareness, are both equally important in climbing. It takes practice and effort to blend them. Improving our ability to listen to our awareness—and listen selectively to our awareness—is critical. We want to marshal our attention, keeping it squarely on the object of intention *while at the same time* remaining open to our awareness and how it informs us about changing environments or subconscious discovery. This listening is somewhat primed by attention as we actively filter out some of the information arising from awareness.

Selecting awareness or attention, therefore, directs the mind to a particular engagement in the world. With the practice of these mechanics, you gain more control, allowing you to consciously pick actions that foster the type of engagement you choose.

Most of the time, since you don't consciously select intention, you end up alternating unconsciously between whatever happens to appear. In the periphery, uneasy feelings and negative thoughts arise while climbing. Sometimes these are indispensable messages requiring our attention, such as the awareness of slightly damp holds, sometimes not. The mindful climber quickly alternates his or her attention from each moment to the next with the full effort given to the skill needed for that moment, without falling prey to phantoms. This mindful alternation is accomplished mostly by keeping the attention high during a movement and then throttling back at any downturns in difficulty, allowing awareness to take over.

Learning to accept and not respond to an unhelpful sub-mind is a skill to practice, yet it's not as simple as blocking out awareness: that's dangerous. It's more about building the correct filtration system so that our attention is not side-tracked unless it really should be. We don't want to take risks we haven't consciously accepted, and we don't want to close ourselves off from our body naturally uncovering a better way to accomplish a sequence than we originally planned. Attention in itself can get so lasered in that is pushes out the wisdom of awareness.

## Attention and Awareness in Balance

While it may seem like you would benefit from 100% attention—hyper-focus—this is rarely the case. Sometimes you benefit from increasing attention; at other times, turning up the dial on awareness helps more. Becoming familiar with how these two sides of consciousness work together enable you to choose the right one for the job.

Fear tends to shut down awareness of everything except what our most basic instincts believe is critical. However, these instincts often lead us astray. For example, I once observed a new leader become captivated by the fears of the sharp end to the point that she became completely unaware of the feeling of the rope crossing the backside of her leg. This created a dangerous situation where a fall would flip her over backward. Her belayer yelled up to her to watch the rope. She didn't respond, overtaken by the immediacy she felt in the moment, focused entirely—too attentive—on how to move upwards. Fortunately, she climbed out of the dangerous position, the rope aligning safely again. However, a few moves higher, the same issue reappeared: the rope ran across the entire backside of her leg from the upper thigh to the outside of her right ankle. Again her belayer meekly cautioned her, "You might want to move your leg," to which she glanced down, then continued trying to find her hand-hold, oblivious to the danger.

Luckily, she completed the route without mishap. After she descended, I mentioned the rope situation to her. She said she was dimly aware of her belayer telling her of the situation, but she never personally felt the rope contact her bare leg, even though it was draped entirely across it. This serves as an example of the importance of distributing consciousness between attention and awareness. The buzz of leading for this particular climber touched off primal instincts, which led her to exclusively focus on what hand-holds she needed to ascend, totally tuned out to the danger.

This example sheds stark light on the necessity of awareness, but the scenario need not be as drastic for awareness to play a significant role in improving as a climber. In general, we can all improve how we open ourselves to awareness. This receptivity takes two forms. The first form is that even while our consciousness is absorbed attending to a single aspect, such as deadpointing a small crimper, we remain open to the sub-minds that send critical feedback. In the previous example, the climber should have been more receptive to the sub-minds warning of potential danger, the result of the feeling of the rope across the back of her leg. This is a kind of passive awareness that we want to continue in the background, even while our focus is laser-tight. The second kind of awareness is more overt, where we consciously release the grip of our brain on specific targets, letting our focus widen both with our eyes and in our mind. This is triggered through the use of the *wide* gaze described in **Chapter 2**.

It's a skill to grant the correct proportion of attention and awareness to a given moment. Some tend to over-emphasize attention as if an entire route is optimally one iron-willed focused effort. It rarely, if ever, is. The subconscious, intuitive, faster awareness is vital in its own right. Learning how to alternate between the two augments our climbing.

## System 1 and System 2

The second model of the mind we turn to in the pursuit of understanding the psyche in climbing is *System 1 and System 2* (also known as the *dual-process* model). Like the previous framework, this also splits mental processes in half:

1. System 1 is the **fast, intuitive**, subconscious, and "easy" mental pathway. We associate this way of thinking with the body or the "gut." It does not require working memory. This forms the vast majority of "thinking" activities. It operates in the background outside of control. The answer to the question "what is 2 + 2" results from System 1 thinking for educated adults, as does reaching back and dipping your hand into your chalk bag most of the time.

2. The System 2 way of thinking is the **slower, analytic, effortful,** and more conscious thought process. This is the mental process we associate with "thinking" as when we chart our trip across town to avoid traffic or solve a long division math problem. It requires the engagement of working memory. Climbing faster than usual for you engages this mentality, as does carefully piecing together a possible way to solve a boulder problem as you look at it from the ground.

These two mental pathways work in conjunction seamlessly most of the time. System 1 keeps raising options to System 2, which usually accepts them without hesitation. This *often* works out fine, resulting in taking action based entirely on the System 1 network. The default outlook of the mind, System 1, is the mental version of auto-pilot. It is characterized by an easy self-confidence, quickly handling the many decisions and actions in our life without reflection or pause.

A classic example of the speedy workings of System 1, as described by Kahneman, suggests the limitations of this way of thinking. Read the following puzzle and answer quickly[2]:

**A bat and ball cost $1.10**

**The bat costs one dollar more than the ball**

**How much does the ball cost?**

The answer that comes to mind quickly is 10¢, illustrating the quick yet wrong tendency of System 1 thinking. In the background, System 1 takes the path of least resistance to an answer: if it looks like a duck and quacks like a duck, then it's a duck. But if you slow down and work out the math using System 2, you calculate the correct answer: 5¢.[3] This takes more cognitive effort and time. Sometimes, it looks and quacks like a duck, but is an alligator in disguise. System 1 falls for this sort of ruse: it's naive. With closer scrutiny and effort via System 2 thinking, we uncover the deception. In short, System 1 is fast and cheap but error-prone while System 2 slower and more costly of mental resource, but more accurate.

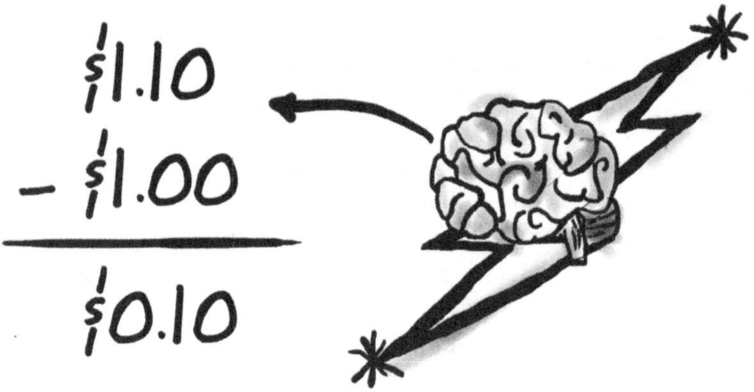


Fast System 1 is easily fooled, but certain it's correct

The analytical mind—System 2—acts more slowly than the body. The more conscious our thoughts, the slower (and more analytical) it becomes. System 2 is effortful and even slightly painful. To demonstrate, see if you

[2] *Khaneman, p. 69.* If you got the answer correct the first time, notice how much you had to slow down in order to come up with it—you actually engaged System 2.

[3] *If the ball is 5¢ and the bat is $1.05 then the total is $1.10 and the bat is $1.00 more than the ball.*

can detect the slight resistance and discomfort with this question: "what is 13 x 3?" It's likely that you even skipped calculating the product even while you read the problem, as we avoid System 2 thought when possible. We often choose to avoid even minor engagements with System 2. Moreover, if you slowed down to do the simple math, it's likely that you double or even triple-checked your answer: System 2 is trepidatious, wary, and cautious. Ironically, we innately feel very certain about the pronouncement of System 1 even though it is error-prone, while the more accurate System 2 evokes insecurity.

In climbing, we usually don't have enough time to operate in System 2. The careful analysis deriving from this mental model is often the worst path while moving. The slower System 2 brain tends to waste precious physical reserves while ascending unless the physical output is low enough to support it. On the other hand, while System 1 thinking is generally the mode we want while moving up route, it sometimes leads us astray. It's a snap judgment about how to solve each movement problem. If the terrain is challenging, the benefits of the fast intuitions gleaned by System 1 *usually* outweigh the seems-right-but-is-wrong results of the mental shorthand wrought by it. Most of the time, the speed, fluidity, and self-certainty are more than worth the cost of small errors in judgment.

Moreover, the self-certainty of the System 1 mindset helps keep us snappy and fluid—we don't bog down into analysis paralysis. While climbing, it is typically true that perfection is the enemy of the good. System 1 often grants a good, if a perhaps imperfect solution to a movement problem—and it does so decisively and quickly. Therefore, System 1 should be the default mentality in ascent.

While the intuition of System 1 should be the standard mental mode while climbing, it has its downsides. As we've seen with the bat and ball puzzle, System 1 falls for trivial and easily avoidable traps. And—even worse—*it smugly thinks it is correct.* This over-confidence should give climbers who rely nearly exclusively on their intuition pause. It's almost a near certainty that they fall prey to the seductive yet flawed product of System 1. They rarely question what "feels right," taking their gut as the sole arbiter of truth while they climb. While a lot of these errors are innocuous, some lead to failure.

## Staying in System 1

- **Stay engrossed.** Keep yourself on task and your attention on the climb. If you start to wander, pick a meta-skill from **Chapter 2** or **3** to execute.
- **Don't engage in System 2 patterns.** If you don't engage in System 2 thought processes such as double-checking your intuitions, your mind tends to stay in the System 1 lane. Don't ask "what if" questions while moving. Save them for pauses. When moving, act decisively.
- **Lighten your mood.** System 1 associates with levity and ease. Small things such as smiling or laughing at yourself promote System 1.

Engaging System 2 would help alleviate some of these wrong turns, but we don't want the downsides of that mode of thought. While it's true that it's often not worth the cost to engage System 2, there are scenarios where it's advantageous:

1. **Before starting a route.** Planning on the ground is a great way to harness the positive aspects of the slower analytical mind as we have all the time in the world to indulge it.
2. **After finishing a route.** When we complete a climb, we can *reflect* on the effort to analyze performance for information that can help us in future ascents.
3. **At intra-route pause stances**, when the climbing eases, we can engage in planning how we will proceed (discussed in **Chapter 6**).

Thinking through a past climb while on the ground with the slower analysis of System 2 may uncover snafus of System 1. When you enjoin System 2, you become more vigilant, suspicious, analytic, and effortful.[4] These traits assist in unearthing movement issues after the fact, training the System 1 mind to look for these patterns on its own, helping you with future ascents. Additionally, talking with partners you trust, or videoing yourself

[4]*Khaneman, p. 69.*

points you down avenues where your System 1 thinking left you blind to glitches. The practice of movements you corrected through reflection is a pivotal way to help bake in more optimal movement solutions you uncover via System 2.

When you are preparing for an on-sight attempt, System 2 is a great way to plan options as you piece together sequences with your eyes before starting. Asking yourself, "well, what if that doesn't go well?" as you look up-route, helps engage System 2 thinking, as does getting very specific about how, *precisely*, you will move through the next four holds after the obvious jug at the third bolt, for example. If, while formulating your plan, you find yourself glossing over part of the route, not paying attention to the details, walk it backward in your mind, replaying that section. The mind wants to skip the effortful detailed stepwise walk of careful analysis. When you choose to engage System 2, keep on top of it and think analytically. It's hard work. If it feels comfortable, you likely lapsed back to System 1.

At intra-route pauses, we can sometimes afford to inspect the route analytically, planning forward progress. If we don't take intra-route breaks to plan when they allow this mental switch, then gullible System 1 may charge headlong into dead ends or waste energy on sub-optimal movement solutions. Conscious switching between these two modes, when an intra-route pause allows, grants us the optimal blend of both ways of thinking. The goal is to remain intuitive until breaks good enough to analytically plan or carefully recall beta.

The two mentalities are not a binary either/or. It takes a lot more System 2 to solve a calculus problem than it does to climb faster than is normal for you. It requires a lot of System 2 to tease out your best guess solution to a crux with a few alternates while looking up at it from an intra-route pause a meter below.

While climbing, the trick is to match the available mental bandwidth, the need for more analytical thought, and the terrain. If we have a lot of time and resource because we are at a large rest and our mind is fresh, then we could choose to plumb the depths of System 2 to look analytically up the route. On the other hand, if the stance is not so great, then just a glance at a key target is all we might have the resource. In these marginal moments, it's often a good idea to stay in System 1. Practice and reflection help you gain wisdom in this regard. It's a sign of improved craftsmanship on your part to discover when and when not to engage System 2.

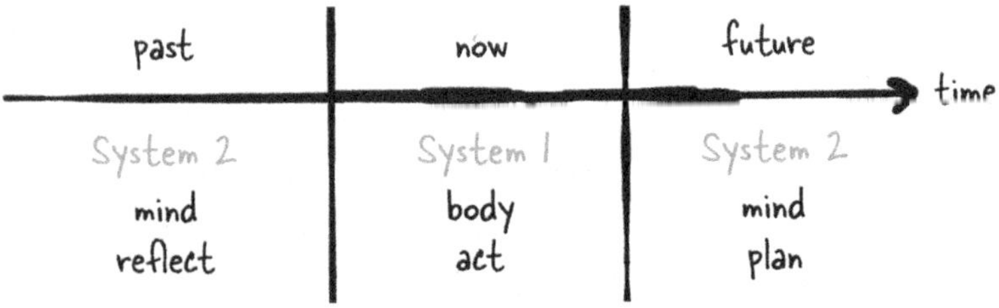


With repetitive, focused practice, some skills transform from effortful System 2 to innate System 1. For example, through practice, movements like powering through a drop-knee, which took a lot of System 2 as you first learned them, fade to the intuitive background, becoming the domain of System 1 as you gain proficiency. While it still requires mindful *attention*, it no longer enters the mentally effortful and timid sphere of System 2. This sheds light on the distinction between *attention* and *System 2* thought. Focusing attention squarely on a mechanic such as a tricky drop knee is not the same as thinking analytically about it, just as driving in chaotic traffic demands full attention even though you aren't enlisting System 2 at the wheel. Practice transforms some tasks from System 2 to 1, but it doesn't also necessarily convert it from one requiring attention to one just in the sphere of awareness.

**Don't mix moving with planning: do one or the other.**

While we can mutate some skills that used to require System 2 to System 1 with focused practice, not all are amenable. For example, it will forever take both focused attention and full engagement with System 2 to carefully evaluate movement options for a crux sequence on your on-sight attempts. We can't train that skill down into intuition. Moreover, it will always feel uncomfortable to engage System 2 in these moments. We will want to avoid it or cut the process short, particularly when the mind or body is exhausted. We tend to overestimate the attention we send to the object of our intention. We think we are directing more resources to System 2 than we are. Knowing this tendency, we need to double our efforts to think carefully and truly engage System 2 when we choose it. Know that it takes effort and will to overcome our avoidance of effortful analytical thought, even when we know it best for the situation. Fully give yourself to it if you decide it's worth the switch.

With this knowledge, you can help yourself by recognizing and countermanding this avoidance when it comes up. Say you ascend thirty feet up a difficult hand crack to a stem rest. The fatigue you feel at that moment will multiply the natural resistance to using that pause to look closely via System 2 at the next chance—and the exact details—to place gear. It's easy to glance up and get an *impression*—that's System 1 at work—it's much harder to get very *specific* and *concrete* about the moves and actions to come.

You can help yourself in these moments by knowing this resistance is just the way of the mind. One possible way to counteract the tendency to avoid System 2 thought when it's a perfect time to use it is perhaps saying to yourself, "Oh this feeling of not wanting to figure out the next sequence while at this rest is just my brain. I'm going to take the time to really think this through anyhow because I know it helps me reach my goal. How, exactly, will I get myself in position to place this cam?" Or, when faced with attempting to solve an intricate series of foot moves, you walk through your best guess quite explicitly like "left front point to the acorn, then right up to the pocket, then left high step on the yoke." *Specificity* in these moments is vital.

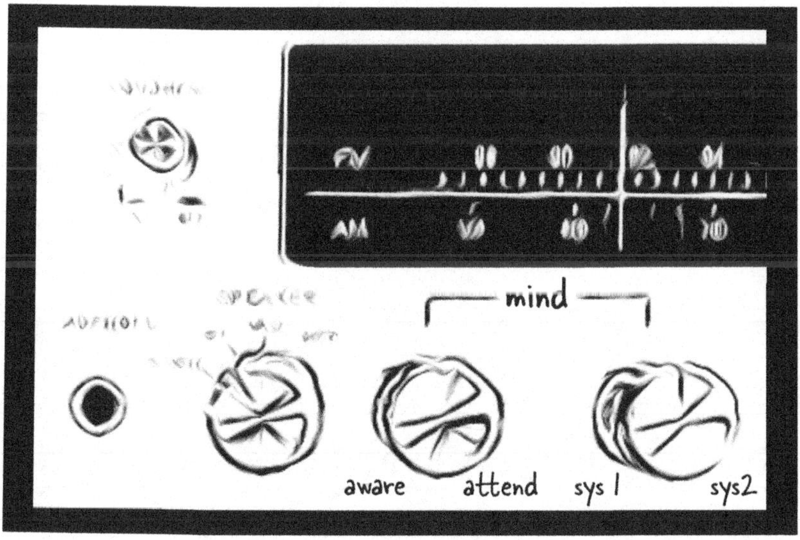

Kevin started climbing in 1991. He resides in Portland, Oregon with his wife Jenn and his son, Tristan.

Made in the USA
Las Vegas, NV
30 April 2024

89335224R00095